THE UNSHACKLED PRESCRIPTION

THE UNSHACKLED PRESCRIPTION

How YOU Can Fix American Healthcare

Rahul Anand

NEW DEGREE PRESS
COPYRIGHT © 2021 RAHUL ANAND
All rights reserved.

THE UNSHACKLED PRESCRIPTION
How YOU Can Fix American Healthcare

ISBN
978-1-63676-829-8   *Paperback*
978-1-63730-213-2   *Kindle Ebook*
978-1-63730-273-6   *Digital Ebook*

CONTENTS

| | DO YOU SINCERELY WANT TO UNDERSTAND AMERICAN HEALTHCARE? | 11 |

PART 1. **HOW WE GOT HERE** — **23**

CHAPTER 1 HOW AMERICAN HEALTHCARE STARTED 25

CHAPTER 2 TWENTY-FIRST-CENTURY GOVERNMENTAL INTERVENTION 47

CHAPTER 3 THE THEORY OF *AUTONOMY* 57

CHAPTER 4 A MULTIDIMENSIONAL APPROACH TO PATIENT AUTONOMY 63

CHAPTER 5 CASE STUDY—PATIENT AUTONOMY 79

CHAPTER 6 HEALTH SYSTEM IN FLUX 85

PART 2. **STANDARDS OF A TOP-TIER HEALTHCARE SYSTEM** — **97**

CHAPTER 7 THE CERTAINTY EPIDEMIC 99

CHAPTER 8 ACHIEVING OPENNESS AND NATIONAL DISCUSSION 109

CHAPTER 9 PRINCIPLES OF A VALUE-BASED SYSTEM 127

PART 3.	**TANGIBLE RESOLUTIONS**	**141**
CHAPTER 10	A PAINFUL PILL TO SWALLOW	143
CHAPTER 11	A PRIMER ON HEALTH INSURANCE	157
CHAPTER 12	THE AFFORDABILITY SCALE	171
CHAPTER 13	WHAT YOU CAN DO TO FIX THE HEALTHCARE SYSTEM AS A PATIENT	185
	CONCLUSION	197
	ACKNOWLEDGMENTS	201
	APPENDIX	203

INTRODUCTION

DO YOU SINCERELY WANT TO UNDERSTAND AMERICAN HEALTHCARE?

A gray day provides the best light.
—LEONARDO DA VINCI

CHARTING THE JOURNEY

CONGRATULATIONS!
Just by opening up this copy of *The Unshackled Prescription*, you have taken an important step to understanding healthcare on the fundamental level.

Growing up in a Hindustani family, this familiar parable eloquently informs us of the current state of healthcare.

A group of blind men heard a strange animal, the elephant, had been brought to town. None of them were aware of the shape or form of the animal. Out of curiosity, they asserted, "We must inspect through touch, of which we are capable." As they sought this, they groped about the elephant. The first person with their hand on the trunk described the elephant as a "thick snake." Another touching the ear argued the complexion of a fan. Yet another touching the leg proposed a tree trunk–like appearance. Placing his hand on the side of the elephant, one blind man said it was a wall. The other blind man grabbed the tail and described it as a rope. The last of the men held the tusk, stating a spear-like description.

No matter our current involvement in healthcare, whether it be as a provider (doctor, nurse, technician), healthcare executive (insurance, pharmaceuticals, hospital management), politician, or as a patient, there is a critical need for a guide that illuminates the gray area of healthcare. As you will come to know, within healthcare there is no absolutely correct approach, especially with subjective experiences limited to one or a few constrained domains.

Most of the guides to understanding healthcare are far disconnected with what the typical patient goes through, and I believe this has played an important role in the entanglements that have grown since the inception of American healthcare. As a former patient myself and a premedical student on the path to study medicine, it is my conviction that this book will be an easy-to-implement guide filled with information that is boiled down to the bottom line, entertaining personal encounters within healthcare and insight from the vanguards of healthcare across various domains.

This book will provide you with the tangible tools to understand American healthcare as a gradient of varying truths and ultimately to navigate healthcare through derived inspiration from various successful international models such as in Singapore.

A DIAGNOSTIC FIASCO

I gleaned over EPIC, a cloud-based emergency health recording (EHR) software used to catalog patient health data, and saw my team's red color filled to the brim. Another physician in the doctor pod of the emergency department had handed off the incoming patients on his chart as his shift was ending. To say the least, there was considerable pressure to proceed through the rounds swiftly. Dr. Smith had just returned from a private consultation, and we were headed off to meet Isabella.

> *Alright, Isabella—before we start our consult, meet Rahul. He will be taking some notes of our conversation, as a scribe. So, tell me, Isabella, what seems to be the main concern you have that has brought you here?*
>
> *Well, I have a stiff neck and a severe headache.*
>
> *And how would you rate your neck ache and headache on a scale of one to ten, with one being mild and ten being the worst pain?*
>
> *I would say a seven for both. Is this anything I should be worried about? Could this be a sign of fever? Muscle tension? Dehydration?*

> *Well, before we get to the exact diagnosis, I would like to ask you a couple of questions about your pain. First, tell me, when did your pain start?*
>
> *My neck pain and headache began last week late evening after I was sitting on my Adirondack chair in my porch.*

Taking notes on my pad, I could notice her pace of words was rather unusual. Even for an elderly woman, it was rather slow.

> *Were you doing any physical exertion, or were you essentially sedentary?*
>
> *Definitely sedentary. I hardly did anything that could be considered exertion.*
>
> *Have you traveled recently? If so, where and for how long?*
>
> *Not recently, no. I have been in town for the past several months.*

Dr. Smith continued probing Isabella on a myriad of other personal details.

> *Well, thank you, Isabella, for sharing this information. I will go ahead and order an X-ray.*

Upon leaving Isabella's room:

> *Dr. Smith, did you find it rather unusual how slow Isabella was speaking?*

> *No, she is quite elderly. Oh, Dr. Hayashi, about the patient in room fifty-seven—I ordered the consult.*

It was 10:57 p.m., and Dr. Smith shared the X-ray results:

> *There are no concerning signs. Likely, it is a muscle sprain. I will discharge Isabella with some pain medications.*

I marked Isabella for discharge.

> *Glad we're one patient down from this bottomless stack.*

The next morning, going through the routine, I was a little perplexed when I saw Isabella's name reappear on EPIC.

> *That's odd. Isabella's back? Come, Rahul—let's see what we have here.*

Walking into room thirty-four, the paramedics shared the details as I copiously typed the information into the EHR.

> *Isabella has had cardiac arrest.*

The paramedics were performing CPR in the resuscitation room.

> *Is it possible that I overlooked the headache? Could that have contributed to Isabella's stroke?* Dr. Smith pondered.

Dr. Smith then proceeded to further examine Isabella and became convinced that the stroke could have been avoided. Isabella was placed on a heart monitor, and a CT scan was ordered. Unfortunately, Isabella's condition deteriorated further, and, despite efforts, Isabella could not be resuscitated.

The physician broke the news to Isabella's family: Isabella was pronounced dead. The physician delicately explained the cause of this seemingly unexpected result. After the conversation with Isabella's family, we went back to the station with the other physicians.

> *I knew it. We should have ordered a CT Friday evening,* Dr. Smith lamented.

WHY THIS BOOK?

This encounter, albeit very unfortunate, is prevalent across the United States. Our healthcare system is failing every day for all. Isabella had come from an impoverished background and, despite coming to a very well-known hospital, was still unable to receive effective treatment for her medical complaints. She had avoided going to her primary care physician due to lack of insurance and then was misdiagnosed in the ED due to pressure on doctors to get to the next patient.

I am deeply passionate about increasing access to healthcare, especially from a health policy and entrepreneurial perspective. During my undergraduate studies, I conducted a lot of clinical research where I got to see the health disparities firsthand and saw how the translation of research to clinical practice involved health disparities based on socioeconomic and various other factors. This inspired me to start the Waterfall Academy and the corresponding Breaking Barriers organization to increase volunteerism for students with autism spectrum disorder (ASD) and to lead a project through Roosevelt Policy Network on reducing pharmaceutical pricing for low-income geriatric populations in urban Texas areas. With COVID-19 halting a lot of the work I was doing, I got involved with the Coronavirus Visualization Team based at Harvard and had the opportunity to work directly with leaders at the United Nations, African Union, and the European Union on policy designs for increasing access to quality and relevant information on COVID-19 in a timely fashion through the creation of spatiotemporal maps, a skill I gained through working with Dr. Kim as an undergraduate research assistant at Duke and UT Southwestern. It was these conversations with healthcare executives, politicians, medical doctors, and countless patients that inspired me to write a self-help guide on understanding the healthcare system, especially during the difficult times throughout COVID-19.

Although a thorough understanding of medical technology is imperative to the success of the modern medical practice, individualized attention to patients is of utmost need. Physicians ought to act in the best interest of the patient and not in favor of the healthcare administration to quickly process patient queues. Both healthcare systems and insurance setups need to come together and improvise to avoid reoccurrence of such instances.

The only high-income country that does not have universal healthcare coverage is the United States. In order to have quality healthcare without financial burden, universal healthcare coverage is of utmost necessity. There have been several attempts at increasing healthcare accessibility. Namely, in 2010, the Patient Protection and Affordable Care Act (ACA) led to notable reductions in the number of people who were uninsured. Despite this, approximately 30 million people remain uninsured, and millions more are underinsured.[1]

Why? In brief, congressional policy decisions. For instance, eligibility for premium tax credits and assistance for cost sharing have been reduced to people who earn less than 400 percent of the federal poverty level.[2] The ACA is politically contentious, and this undermines its viability.

There is a common misconception that spending more improves quality. However, this is certainly not the case with healthcare. The United States spends more on healthcare per capita than any other high-income country, and spending is on the rise.[3] The next logical question becomes: why is healthcare so costly in the United States?

According to a study performed by the National Health Expenditure Accounts Team, 33 percent of the spending comes from hospital services, 20 percent from clinical services, and 9 percent from prescription drugs.[4] However, this is not simply a

---

[1] "Key Facts about the Uninsured Population," *KFF*, accessed August 27, 2020.

[2] Ibid.

[3] "U.S. Health Care from a Global Perspective, 2019: Higher Spending, Worse Outcomes?" *The Commonwealth Fund*, accessed August 30, 2020.

[4] "CMS Office of the Actuary Releases 2018 National Health Expenditures," *Centers for Medicare & Medicaid Services*, accessed August 18, 2020.

matter of healthcare being expensive to maintain. Japan has a similar population size and, as a member of the Organization for Economic Cooperation and Development (OECD), is a high-income country. Japan spends less than half of what the United States spends per capita on healthcare.[5] Moreover, based on OECD data, people in the United States are not using healthcare any more than other high-income countries.[6]

The spending difference is due to the high prices in the United States. A recent study by PwC Health Research Institute showed that spending more does not equate to improved productivity or health in the United States.[7] A study in Cambridge, UK, showed that nearly 80 percent of a person's health can be attributed to socioeconomic factors, health behaviors, and their physical environment.[8] If a person lives in a food swamp that has greater access to fast-food restaurants and other stores that lack nutritious food, said person would have a higher risk for obesity. Hence, it is important to recognize if the complex set of factors that contribute to healthcare spending are not addressed, the United States will continue to experience excessive spending without any measurable health improvements.

---

5   "How does health spending in the U.S. compare to other countries?" *Peterson-KFF Health System Tracker*, accessed August 23, 2020.

6   Ibid.

7   "What's likely to drive medical cost trend in 2019?" *PWC United States*, accessed August 22, 2020.

8   Paula Braveman and Laura Gottlieb, "The Social Determinants of Health: It's Time to Consider the Causes of the Causes," *Public Health Reports* 129, no. 2 (2014): 19-31.

However, much can be learned from abroad. What is truly special about the Singaporean healthcare system is the delivery—how payment is made. Nearly 80 percent of Singaporeans receive low-cost primary care through the private sector.[9] The remaining 20 percent use polyclinics that are run by the government.[10] Polyclinics serve as an option when care becomes increasingly expensive and complex. The design is a marvel of efficiency. Emphasis is placed on processing a maximum of patients. However, hospitalizations have a flipped situation. Twenty percent use private hospitals, and 80 percent use public hospitals that are heavily subsidized.[11] Hence, Singapore does not have a private healthcare system; it is simply privately funded. Singapore, thus, has a large privately funded public delivery system.[12] This is the opposite of how funding is in the United States, where a publicly financed private delivery system is utilized.

In this book, I share novel tactics to navigate the American healthcare system through my conversations with current well-regarded leaders in the healthcare industry such as Dr. Thomas Frieden, former director of the CDC; Dr. Mario Molina, CEO of Molina Healthcare; Dr. Paul Rothman, CEO of Johns Hopkins Medicine; and Dr. Stephen Sonnenberg, a professor of medical education at UT Austin Dell Medical School.

---

9   "International Health Care System Profiles Singapore," *The Commonwealth Fund*, accessed July 05, 2020.

10 Ibid.

11 "International Health Care System Profiles Singapore," *The Commonwealth Fund*, accessed July 05, 2020.

12 Ibid.

Perhaps the most important lesson I share in this book is to understand the big picture. I share the roles of various healthcare players: patients, providers (doctors, nurses, technicians), healthcare executives (insurance companies, pharmaceuticals), and politicians.

My hope is that after reading this book, you will be able to have a thorough enough understanding of the highly complex American healthcare system to navigate the healthcare system to advocate for yourself, your loved ones, and perhaps the larger patient community through your actions.

In order to translate similar results in the US healthcare system as those found in Singapore, the first priority of policymakers should be increasing patient knowledge. Once a vast majority of patients have a heightened understanding of what their role in the healthcare system is, then there can be an effective collaboration with other key players in the healthcare system. There is a need to understand how bills are made, how financing is currently done, how financing can be improved, and how patients can play an active role in this shift from high costs and poor quality of care to a system that capitalizes on the role of patients for a low-cost system with high quality of care.

PART I

HOW WE GOT HERE

CHAPTER 1

HOW AMERICAN HEALTHCARE STARTED

1546 COLLECTION—UNDERSTANDING THE BIG PICTURE

You can't see the wood for the trees.[13]

A well-known epigram now, it was coined by John Heywood in the 1546 collection. This epigram cannot hold any more truth for healthcare, which is filled with entanglements that make it difficult to understand the big picture.

In this section, I will outline the American healthcare system from its inception with the hope to serve this epigram well.

If one is to look at the best healthcare systems in the world, one is likely to find countries such as Canada, Germany, Japan, and Singapore. It is important to understand how such lists

---

13 *Cambridge Dictionary*, s.v. "can't see the wood for the trees," accessed September 28, 2020.

are compiled. There are five main criteria: the costs of care, quality of care, accessibility, overall health of the population, and the up-front costs.

EARLY DAYS

In 1765, the first medical college was established in Philadelphia. Before 1765, doctors were able to practice medicine through experience in what was called the European apprentice system.[14] There were also more ambitious doctors who perfected their medical skills by studying in European medical schools in locations such as London and Paris, among others. William Shippen, Jr., and John Morgan, after completing their medical studies in Europe, established a medical school in Philadelphia, the University of Pennsylvania School of Medicine, and thus established the concept of medical education in the United States.[15] Based on the model of John Morgan, other medical schools were established at universities such as Harvard and Yale.[16] Due to the fact that medical schools became quite popular and therefore profitable, several schools not formally associated with any university also started to become established. Some of these medical schools offered a high level of education, training competent physicians, while others produced subpar graduates.

In the 1700s, there was no requirement to have government licensure in the United States to pursue medicine as a

---

14 Theresa McCulla, "Medicine in Colonial North America," *Colonial North America at Harvard Library*, 2016.

15 Ibid.

16 Theresa McCulla, "Medicine in Colonial North America," *Colonial North America at Harvard Library*, 2016.

profession.[17] Anyone, even those without formal education, could become a physician if they were able to earn the trust of their patients. Patients could also sort out the sheep from the goats by looking for doctors who graduated from prestigious universities and dismissed those doctors who were not graduates of such universities.

An important note is some doctors who did not have a medical degree but practiced with only a master's degree potentially could achieve expertise and therefore be successful through patient recommendations. However, John Farquhar Fulton wrote that as more medical schools were established, a trend of lower education appeared. Interestingly, the proposal to change this state of affairs came from physicians who were medical school graduates and not patients.[18] Physicians lobbied for requirements of legal licensure in medicine.[19] One of the consequences of this was the reduction in the level of competition due to an increased barrier of entry.[20]

In the year 1821, Connecticut authorities began licensure for physicians and forced those who did not have sufficient education to take and pass examinations by the state.[21] Soon

---

17 Ibid.
18 Gordon Shepherd and Cynthia Tsay, "Triumph and Tragedy: The Life of John Farquhar Fulton," *Harvey Cushing/John Hay Whitney Medical Library.*
19 Ibid.
20 Gordon Shepherd and Cynthia Tsay, "Triumph and Tragedy: The Life of John Farquhar Fulton," *Harvey Cushing/John Hay Whitney Medical Library.*
21 Ibid.

other states followed suit.[22] In 1847, the New York Medical Society was established in order to set medical school admission requirements and licensure examinations.[23] This curtailed competition for the already licensed physicians. Licensing caused the supply of medical services to be limited and prices to rise.

Milton Friedman, in his book *Capitalism and Freedom,* cites a perceptive analogy:

> If the government were to suddenly ban all production of cars that were not up to the Cadillac quality, then car quality would surely increase. [24]

However, since neither inferior nor cheaper cars would be produced, for many people buying any car at all would be nearly impossible. This is because some people simply cannot afford a Cadillac, hence removing inferior cars leaves them unable to afford any car. Furthermore, Milton Friedman questioned the very presumption that licenses result in higher healthcare standards. In Friedman's medical licensure conclusion, he wrote:

> When these effects are taken into account, I am myself persuaded that licensure has reduced both the quantity and quality of medical practice; that it has reduced the opportunities available to people who

---

22 Gordon Shepherd and Cynthia Tsay, "Triumph and Tragedy: The Life of John Farquhar Fulton," *Harvey Cushing/John Hay Whitney Medical Library.*

23 Ibid.

24 Milton Friedman, *Capitalism and Freedom* (Chicago: University of Chicago Press, 1962).

would like to be physicians, forcing them to pursue occupations they regard as less attractive; that it has forced the public to pay more for less satisfactory medical service, and that it has retarded technological development both in medicine itself and in the organization of medical practice. I conclude that licensure should be eliminated as a requirement for the practice of medicine.[25]

TWENTIETH-CENTURY HEALTHCARE

Friedman's words can be supported through events later in history. In 1910, Abraham Flexner showed that of the 155 medical schools in the United States and Canada, many were subpar, and the independent institutions were both inferior and not funded adequately, especially when compared to medical schools at universities.[26] Abraham Flexner recommended medical school admission should require at least two years of college education and the medical training should take at least four years.[27] Flexner proposed subpar medical schools should be incorporated into existing universities or they should be shut down.[28]

When his recommendations became law, there was another reduction in the number of physicians. In 1900, there were

---

25   Ibid.

26   Abraham Flexner and Herman Gates Weiskotten, *Flexner Report* (Princeton: Carnegie Foundation for the Advancement of Teaching, 1910).

27   Ibid.

28   Abraham Flexner and Herman Gates Weiskotten, *Flexner Report* (Princeton: Carnegie Foundation for the Advancement of Teaching, 1910).

175 doctors per hundred thousand citizens, whereas in 1930, there were only 125 doctors per hundred thousand citizens.[29] [30] Between 1900 and 1930, over thirty medical schools closed.[31]

This shortage of doctors persisted as a perennial issue. Hence, it is not surprising that in 1932, the Committee on the Costs of American Medical Care issued a report on how to reorganize this sector.[32] In an effort to curtail these rising costs, one proposal was the partitioning of medical care payments through taxing, insurance, or a combination of both of these.[33]

At this point, we will understand how doctors have charged patients over the past few decades. Up to a point, the service and pay relationship was most apparent. However, in addition to this, there were insurance policies that were bought as an auxiliary measure to pay for severe illness hospitalization. Insurance in the early 1900s covered only severe situations rather than routine checkups—analogous to car insurance covering accidents and such, not every bulb or oil change.[34]

---

29 Ibid.

30 Abraham Flexner and Herman Gates Weiskotten, *Flexner Report* (Princeton: Carnegie Foundation for the Advancement of Teaching, 1910).

31 Ibid.

32 "The Final Report of the Committee on the Costs of Medical Care," *New England Journal of Medicine 207* (1932).

33 Ibid.

34 Rosemary A. Stevens, "Health Care in the Early 1960s," *Medicare & Medicaid Research Review* 18, no. 2 (1996).

In the 1930s, being an American doctor was not easy because many times they were paid in home-baked goods.[35] Due to this, doctors working in hospitals were convinced that having their own insurance companies would cover the cost of their services and would serve as an effective solution. However, during this period of hardship—the Great Depression—many citizens were not able to afford routine checkups. This caused hospital insurers to extend their coverage to include routine checkups.[36] In order to avoid premiums from becoming too expensive, the government was asked to aid in this process.[37] BlueCross and BlueShield were established, and thus began the era of the new insurance model.[38]

By obtaining tax exemption, insurance companies set healthcare costs at an acceptable level for the public. The goal was that paying premiums would allow for total coverage of healthcare by insurance companies, including routine checkups. Furthermore, doctors would no longer have to worry about their salaries. Subsequently, the government forced the insurance companies to replace the traditional risk rating for the "community rating." The "community rating" forced insurers to calculate a single premium for every medical plan within a given geographical region without consideration of their client's individual age, sex, or medical history.[39] However,

---

35   Ibid.

36   Rosemary A. Stevens, "Health Care in the Early 1960s," *Medicare & Medicaid Research Review* 18, no. 2 (1996).

37   Ibid.

38   Rosemary A. Stevens, "Health Care in the Early 1960s," *Medicare & Medicaid Research Review* 18, no. 2 (1996).

39   Alan C. Monheit, Joel C. Cantor, Margaret Koller, and Kimberley S. Fox, "Community Rating and Sustainable Individual Health Insurance Markets in New Jersey," *Health Affairs* 23, no. 4 (2004).

through this risk socialization, clients with higher individual risk were rewarded with cheaper premiums compared to clients with low individual risk.[40]

A moral hazard was developed whereby clients could increase their individual risk without exposing themselves to any practical consequence and benefiting in the process. Under an individual risk rating, if you are slim, free of addictions, and exercise every day, you pay a much lower insurance premium than if you are an obese smoker who drinks a lot of alcohol. This lower premium may create a financial incentive to take better care of yourself in order to reduce your insurance costs. However, when costs of treatment for people with unhealthy lifestyles were shared among all insured clients, an opportunity to abuse the system appeared. The financial incentive to take care of yourself disappears. Some people will take higher risks because they will be freed from having to bear the consequences of their actions. This scheme of paying all costs of medical care through the third party, the insurers, is the root of the problem that persists to this day. A vicious cycle that involved moral hazard was created.

Therefore, insurance companies removed individual incentive to reduce cost, hence insurance premiums had to increase, and that prompted the healthiest of clients to terminate their insurance, as for them the costs surpassed the benefits. When clients with the smallest individual risk left, insurance costs had to rise further.

Making this model standard after World War II meant that the client could not negotiate prices with their physician

---

40   Ibid.

anymore.[41] It was no longer possible to compare prices offered by different doctors, which previously favored lower prices.

Milton Friedman proposed four ways in which we spend money.[42] The first way is to spend your own money on yourself.[43] In doing so, there is a high concern for quality and cost so you try to get the most value for your money.[44] The goal here is to get the best quality of care at lower prices.[45] The second way is to spend someone else's money on yourself.[46] In doing so, there is a high concern for quality but a low concern for cost.[47] The third way is to spend your own money on someone else. In doing so, there is a low concern for quality and a high concern for cost.[48] The fourth way is to spend other people's money on someone else.[49] Here, there is a low concern for both the quality and the cost.[50] When paying your physician directly, you

---

41 Alan C. Monheit, Joel C. Cantor, Margaret Koller, and Kimberley S. Fox, "Community Rating and Sustainable Individual Health Insurance Markets in New Jersey," *Health Affairs* 23, no. 4 (2004).

42 Milton Friedman, *Capitalism and Freedom* (Chicago: University of Chicago Press, 1962).

43 Ibid.

44 Milton Friedman, *Capitalism and Freedom* (Chicago: University of Chicago Press, 1962).

45 Ibid.

46 Milton Friedman, *Capitalism and Freedom* (Chicago: University of Chicago Press, 1962).

47 Ibid.

48 Milton Friedman, *Capitalism and Freedom* (Chicago: University of Chicago Press, 1962).

49 Ibid.

50 Milton Friedman, *Capitalism and Freedom* (Chicago: University of Chicago Press, 1962).

act in the first way: you care about both cost and quality. However, in the present system this has changed, as the costs are being paid by the third party—the insurance company—with the premiums based on the community rating. This causes the patient to act in the second way—caring about quality but not cost—while the insurance company acts in the third way—caring about cost but not quality. As can be seen, this makes the interest of the patient and the insurers contradictory.

World War II left its mark on healthcare as well. Due to the fact that a large part of the population fought in Europe, the supply of labor fell sharply. Generally, when supply falls, the price goes up. It was no different with wage rates. To counteract this, in 1942, the US government froze wage rates with the Stabilization Act.[51] Employers were unable to raise wages to compete for employees, so they started to offer additional benefits such as paying for health insurance because the government did not treat this as raising wages.[52] Furthermore, according to the law, employee benefits could be deducted from profits when calculating taxes, thus making them lower for the employer.[53] In contrast, when the employees wanted to buy insurance for themselves, they had to pay with money after tax.[54] This was another step toward the collectivization of healthcare.

---

51 Stephen Mihm, "Employer-based health care was a wartime accident," *Chicago Tribune*, February 24, 2017.

52 Ibid.

53 Stephen Mihm, "Employer-based health care was a wartime accident," *Chicago Tribune*, February 24, 2017.

54 Ibid.

Since only employers who bought group insurance were entitled to tax deductions, this resulted in a relatively small number of companies being insurers for huge groups of people. An additional problem that lingered was that it was harder to transfer insurance policy conditions when changing jobs.[55] If you became chronically ill at one job, then you had to pay higher premiums at your next job.[56] If you already had a binding insurance contract before you lost your health, then as long you kept your old job you paid the same premiums.[57] Years passed and, in the United States, there were more and more elderly people who needed medical care more often.[58] Insurers operating under the community rating system began to suffer financial problems, allowing entry to private insurers that had more freedom in determining premiums.[59] It was not profitable for physicians and hospitals to offer medical care to indigent older people even before this increase of costs, let alone afterwards.[60] As a result of rising costs of medical care, and consequently of snowballing premiums, some older people started to have trouble accessing treatment.[61]

---

55   Stephen Mihm, "Employer-based health care was a wartime accident," *Chicago Tribune*, February 24, 2017.

56   Ibid.

57   Stephen Mihm, "Employer-based health care was a wartime accident," *Chicago Tribune*, February 24, 2017.

58   Ibid.

59   Stephen Mihm, "Employer-based health care was a wartime accident," *Chicago Tribune*, February 24, 2017.

60   Ibid.

61   Stephen Mihm, "Employer-based health care was a wartime accident," *Chicago Tribune*, February 24, 2017.

JOHNSON ADMINISTRATION

In 1965, President Lyndon Johnson signed amendments to the Social Security Act, which, among other measures, established Medicare and Medicaid.[62] Medicare is social health insurance that covers people over age sixty-five as well as some disabled and chronically ill people below this age.[63] Medicaid is a healthcare program for specific people in families with limited income and resources.[64] The establishment of Medicare pulled all people over sixty-five out of the private insurance market.[65] The cost of medical care for older people—who constituted the segment of the population with the highest risk of illness and the highest cost of treatment—fell on the taxpayers.[66] The cost of Medicare rose from 1965 to 1980 because of changing behavior in both medical service providers and patients.[67] The managers of medical institutions knew they would be reimbursed, and hence they expanded their services to meet the rising demand for medical care.[68] Without having to pay directly, patients exploited the system as much as they could.[69] For instance, a patient may insist a provider bill their spouse's insurance knowing well the insurance would deny

---

62 "History of SSA During the Johnson Administration 1963—1968," *Social Security*.

63 Ibid.

64 "History of SSA During the Johnson Administration 1963—1968," *Social Security*.

65 Ibid.

66 "History of SSA During the Johnson Administration 1963—1968," *Social Security*.

67 Ibid.

68 "History of SSA During the Johnson Administration 1963—1968," *Social Security*.

69 Ibid.

payment since their spouse has exceeded their plan limit on that particular treatment for that year.[70] Once the insurance denies the claim, the patient may desire for the provider to negotiate with the insurance plan on their behalf to get the claim paid.[71] There are several things wrong with this.[72] First, a medical provider bills a patient insurance plan as a courtesy, not because it is mandatory.[73] Second, when the billing department employed by the provider loses the claim, they spend a large amount on this entire ordeal.[74]

This exploitation happens from patients, regardless of socio-economic background.

Politicians were eager to control the costs but preferred not to introduce unpopular limits on treatment.[75] Instead, politicians limited payments for medical care.[76] Before that, physicians simply billed Medicare.[77] However, another system based on the diagnosis-related groups (DRGs) was

---

70 "History of SSA During the Johnson Administration 1963—1968," *Social Security.*

71 Ibid.

72 "History of SSA During the Johnson Administration 1963—1968," *Social Security.*

73 Ibid.

74 "History of SSA During the Johnson Administration 1963—1968," *Social Security.*

75 Ibid.

76 "History of SSA During the Johnson Administration 1963—1968," *Social Security.*

77 Ibid.

introduced to solve the problem.[78] In short, the aim of DRGs was to determine in advance how much hospitals should be paid for the treatment of a given disease.[79] In economic terms, it was a system of price controls, and, as is well known by economists, setting maximum prices leads to shortages.[80]

The same goes for medical services. Private insurers also had to adopt DRGs, and, as it concerned hospital treatment, the result was a reduction in the supply of hospital care services and an increase in the supply of outpatient treatment services.[81] The physicians had more freedom when setting payment rates in the case of outpatient treatment.

As mentioned earlier, a reduction in the supply of medical services led to a reduction in the ratio of doctors per number of citizens; and soon there was a shortage of physicians. Some changes in the Social Security Act that established Medicare included subsidies to Graduate Medical Education (GME).[82] Both the students and the hospitals that trained them were subsidized.[83] From 1965 to 1980, teaching hospitals used part of these funds to finance the treatment of their indigent

---

78 Elizabeth Davis, "Diagnostic Related Grouping and How It Works," *verywellhealth,* November 26, 2020.

79 Ibid.

80 Elizabeth Davis, "Diagnostic Related Grouping and How It Works," *verywellhealth,* November 26, 2020.

81 Ibid.

82 "History of SSA During the Johnson Administration 1963—1968," *Social Security.*

83 Ibid.

patients.[84] Beginning in the 1980s, as other hospitals became aware of these subsidies, they started to divert their indigent patients toward the teaching hospitals.[85] The workload in the teaching hospitals related to indigent patients had reached critical levels, even though the resident doctors worked over one hundred hours a week.[86] To add insult to injury, there emerged a practice of private hospitals "dumping indigent patients" at teaching hospitals.[87] Every now and then, even an unstable patient was transferred by a private hospital to a teaching hospital, which was both costly and disturbing to the public.[88]

REAGAN ADMINISTRATION

In 1986, President Ronald Reagan proved both political parties were willing to intervene in the medical market when he signed into law the Emergency Medical Treatment and Active Labor Act (EMTALA), which was part of an even larger congressional Consolidated Omnibus Reconciliation Act (COBRA). EMTALA imposed the following duties on hospitals:[89]

---

84 "History of SSA During the Johnson Administration 1963—1968," *Social Security*.

85 Ibid.

86 "History of SSA During the Johnson Administration 1963—1968," *Social Security*.

87 Ibid.

88 "History of SSA During the Johnson Administration 1963—1968," *Social Security*.

89 Megan Ladd and Vikas Gupta, "Cobra Laws and EMTALA," *StatPearls*, February 16, 2021.

- Emergency rooms had to provide a medical screening exam on anyone who requested it and determine whether they were suitable for an immediate treatment.[90] This had to be done regardless of such person's ability or intention to pay for the exam.[91]

- If the patient was suitable for immediate treatment, the second duty was to stabilize their condition or arrange transport to a hospital that could.[92]

- The transfer of said patient was to be accepted if the hospital had specialized equipment required for a given treatment.[93] Refusal was not an option.[94] This duty also disregarded whether the patient would pay or not.[95]

    – At the same time, the patient had to request such transfer after being informed about its risks and the hospital's duty to stabilize.[96] When such a request was impossible, for example due to a patient's loss of consciousness, the doctor was required to sign a

---

90 Ibid.

91 Megan Ladd and Vikas Gupta, "Cobra Laws and EMTALA," *StatPearls*, February 16, 2021.

92 Ibid.

93 Megan Ladd and Vikas Gupta, "Cobra Laws and EMTALA," *StatPearls*, February 16, 2021.

94 Ibid.

95 Megan Ladd and Vikas Gupta, "Cobra Laws and EMTALA," *StatPearls*, February 16, 2021.

96 Ibid.

certification that the medical benefits of transportation outweighed the risks.[97]

This law has been criticized for its vagueness. For instance, stabilization was defined as "no medical deterioration should occur from or during the transfer."[98] The first legal cases provided to the courts treated these terms so strictly that almost every patient could be considered unstable.[99] The plaintiff did not even need to prove the patient's medical condition had deteriorated.[100] It was enough that the patient's medical condition could deteriorate for a physician or a hospital to be found guilty.[101] The penalties for violating this law were extreme: a $50,000 penalty for each violation, with many violations per patient possible.[102] In addition, compensations paid to the hospital to which the patient was transferred or two-year termination of the Medicare/Medicaid program were also possible.[103] This often meant grave financial problems for the physician or the hospital. EMTALA increased the demand for hospital care just as the DRG reduced the supply.[104] From then on, when a doctor faced a situation, they

---

97 Megan Ladd and Vikas Gupta, "Cobra Laws and EMTALA," *StatPearls*, February 16, 2021.

98 Ibid.

99 Megan Ladd and Vikas Gupta, "Cobra Laws and EMTALA," *StatPearls*, February 16, 2021.

100 Ibid.

101 Megan Ladd and Vikas Gupta, "Cobra Laws and EMTALA," *StatPearls*, February 16, 2021.

102 Ibid.

103 Megan Ladd and Vikas Gupta, "Cobra Laws and EMTALA," *StatPearls*, February 16, 2021.

104 Ibid.

sent the patient to the ER with the certainty someone would take care of them.[105]

Were someone to have a small car accident, the police would advise the patient to go the ER. EMTALA resulted in ERs being treated like free clinics.[106] Murphy and McGuff, authors of *The Primal Prescription*, compared it to an overflowing bathtub.[107] While the DRGs acted as the drain plug that prevented patients (water) from exiting, EMTALA turned the faucet on full blast.[108] As a result of the financial costs imposed by EMTALA, the ERs and hospitals around the country were being shut down.[109] The survivors suffered from a shortage of subspecialty on-call backup.

EMTALA also resulted in costs being shifted around. When free clinics, hospitals, and doctors started to sue ERs and tried to recoup their losses by charging higher fees to the clients who paid, the regulations made the profession increasingly burdensome for the doctors because of all the red tape.[110] The physician had to fill an ever-increasing pile of documents to receive refunds for the services rendered. Even hopes of solving the issue with the use of computers was for naught, as their introduction was coercive instead of voluntary.

---

105 Megan Ladd and Vikas Gupta, "Cobra Laws and EMTALA," *StatPearls*, February 16, 2021.

106 Ibid.

107 Megan Ladd and Vikas Gupta, "Cobra Laws and EMTALA," *StatPearls*, February 16, 2021.

108 Ibid.

109 Megan Ladd and Vikas Gupta, "Cobra Laws and EMTALA," *StatPearls*, February 16, 2021.

110 Ibid.

According to Doug McGuff, while such functions as prescription-writing and patient-discharge procedures were an important component, the charting took much more time. Using the old approach, he wrote, "I could see patients at almost double the pace."[111] In the case of a computer malfunction, the entire department could cease to function, which posed a great threat to the dynamic environment of the ER.

The FDA is responsible for controlling the pharmaceutical industry, among various other tasks. According to McGuff and Murphy:

> On the one hand, it prolongs the development of potentially useful drugs, leading to delayed treatment and artificially inflated prices. On the other hand, the FDA also fails to protect Americans from unacceptably dangerous drugs, even when experts in the private sector have raised alarm bells. [112]

OBAMA ADMINISTRATION

Hence, it can be observed that the price increase was caused by various interventions made in the market—where some involved increasing demands for particular medical services and some reducing the supply of medical services.

There is no doubt the problem of rising healthcare costs existed prior to the Affordable Care Act (ACA). Moreover,

---

[111] Doug McGuff and Robert P. Murphy, *Primal Prescription: Surviving the "Sick Care" Sinkhole* (Oxnard: Primal Blueprint Publishing, 2015).

[112] Ibid.

many have claimed the free market has failed to provide ACA, and this is simply false since historical evidence has clearly shown that people have not been allowed to act freely.

It is worth noting that in 2010, when President Obama signed the ACA into law, this was not designed to be a healthcare reform.[113] It was entirely about health insurance. It is also important to note that American health insurance is not an insurance per se, since it covers *all* events instead of only sudden, expensive, and unexpected ones.

Imagine how expensive home insurance would be if home insurance covered minutia such as replacing light bulbs and sink repairs. As a result, such insurance ceases being an insurance and rather becomes a different means of paying for all costs of maintaining a house with added premiums for unexpected events.

Analogously, a doctor visit for a cold is like having a sink repair in a home. Neither is unexpected, and both are quick repairs financially. The problem, however, is US health insurance does not fully cover the costs of serious, unforeseen cases and rather requires from the insured a partial cost coverage, which at times is not possible.

Overarchingly, the ACA provided a mechanism to allow most Americans to have:[114]

---

113 Kimberly Amadeo, "What is Obamacare?" *The Balance*, September 17, 2020.

114 Ibid.

- Coverage;

- Community rating (nondiscriminatory pricing in premiums);

- Essential health benefits (minimum standards for health plans);

- Government subsidies for the economically disadvantaged;

- Several taxes on the wealthy to pay for the new spending commitments;

- Government guarantees for the health insurance companies;

- Employer mandate (a requirement that some employers would provide health insurance for some of their employees); and

- Individual mandate (a requirement that nearly everyone has health insurance).

CONCLUSION

- The criteria for evaluating healthcare systems are: costs of care, quality of care, accessibility, overall health of the population, and the up-front costs.

- Medical licensing caused the supply of medical services to be limited and prices to rise.

- The "community rating" forced insurers to calculate a single premium for every medical plan within a given geographical region without consideration of their client's individual age, sex, or medical history. However, through this risk socialization, clients with higher individual risk were rewarded with cheaper premiums compared to clients with low risk.

- A moral hazard was developed whereby clients could increase their individual risk without exposing themselves to any practical consequence and benefiting in the process. This scheme of paying all costs of medical care through the third party, the insurers, is the root of the problem that persists to this day. When clients with smallest individual risk left, insurance costs had to rise further.

- In the present system the costs are being paid by the third party—the insurance company—with the premiums based on the community rating. This causes the patient to care about quality but not cost while the insurance company cares about cost but not quality. This makes the interests of the patient and the insurers contradictory. This exploitation happens from patients, regardless of socioeconomic background.

- The current state of American healthcare is like imagining how expensive home insurance would be if home insurance covered minutia such as replacing light bulbs and sink repairs. As a result, such insurance ceases being an insurance and instead becomes a different means of paying for all costs related to maintaining a house plus added premiums for unexpected events.

CHAPTER 2

TWENTY-FIRST-CENTURY GOVERNMENTAL INTERVENTION

Twenty-first-century healthcare presents a complex problem. There has been major progress through technological advancements; however, the traditional structure of the American healthcare system is crumbling. For instance, clearly there are a lot more therapeutic options for a vast number of medical conditions; however, this is accompanied by the amount and diversity of individuals involved in the care delivery process. This results in medical providers experiencing collaboration issues, patients experiencing difficulty in navigating the healthcare system, and leaders who are unable to lead properly due to this.

There were several consequences accompanying these regulation implementations. Aside from the obvious replacement of the free will of people with greater state power and governmental market interference, *universal* coverage was a motivation from the understanding that prices for insurance had skyrocketed due to the interventions discussed earlier and that a substantial number of Americans were unable to afford even basic coverage. By the year 2009, nearly 50 million individuals did not have health insurance at all.[115]

The ACA does not insinuate utter nationalization of medical care, and the private sector is still able to provide health insurance. Theoretically speaking, government intervention is merely designed such that all individuals are covered. Regulations accompanied a domino effect. Once the ACA was enacted, insurance companies could try to find a means of doing their job at the expense of quality. This is why regulations, such as minimum standards and community ratings, were so important to implement in health plans.

Since young, healthy people pay for patients covered by insurance below cost, it became necessary to implement insurance obligations to prevent their flight from the system. The question then became, what could be done when such burdens became excessive? The solution was simply to tax the wealthy to subsidize others.[116] Hence, as can be observed, after every regulation, there came the consequent need to introduce another and another.

---

115 Kimberly Amadeo, "What is Obamacare?" *The Balance*, September 17, 2020.

116 Ibid.

Effectively, the ACA was 906 pages long, and the expenses related to this bill since its introduction have amounted to around $1 trillion.[117]

The problem with community rating is the incorrect underlying assumption that people are identical in health status, and this ends up harming those who actually take care of their own health. Currently, the only features allowed to affect insurance rates are place of residence, age, smoking, and family size.[118] Despite this constraint on insurers, there is a ban on freely setting premiums.[119] For instance, insurers are limited to charging the elderly up to three times that of their younger counterparts. This is a drop from a previous ratio of five to one, respectively.[120] Through this, there is a property redistribution from those who are healthier to those are unhealthy and from younger to older individuals. The ACA has expanded this redistribution scope.

The community rating also affects moral hazard. When insurers are prevented from requesting higher premiums for risk factors associated with an unhealthy lifestyle, there is, in essence, a discouragement of taking care of one's own health, and thereby the future costs of treating such patients rises over time.

---

[117] Alan C. Monheit, Joel C. Cantor, Margaret Koller, and Kimberley S. Fox, "Community Rating and Sustainable Individual Health Insurance Markets in New Jersey," *Health Affairs* 23, no. 4, (2004).

[118] Ibid.

[119] Alan C. Monheit, Joel C. Cantor, Margaret Koller, and Kimberley S. Fox, "Community Rating and Sustainable Individual Health Insurance Markets in New Jersey," *Health Affairs* 23, no. 4, (2004).

[120] Ibid.

Through an introduction of minimum standards for health plans, limits on spending for essential benefits were established. These minimal standards included many absurdities. For instance, after menopause women were mandated to buy insurance that covered maternity leave.[121] This constituted redistribution, such that women who would not go on maternity leave subsidized women who would go on maternity leave. Accordingly, when people were given the option of buying insurance only for critical condition situations and to pay for routine visits to their provider up to a certain amount, they would have a strong incentive to avoid such visits simply by being more careful. However, this incentive is retracted when more expensive plans are imposed. As a result, the moral hazard was increased.

The goal was to imprison those in the system who were in a better position financially without it. Insurance was expected to not become affordable in any way.

There are substantial effects in virtually every situation when discussing subsidies and benefits for the indigent. Hence, subsidizing indigent individuals is an important incentive for people who are marginal to give up their low-paying occupations and to live on the subsidies. In this particular case, more people will entirely depend on the state in regard to their medical care. Since these subsidizes are targeted at individuals who earn low incomes, their incentive is simply to avoid earning higher incomes by doing more efficient work, and this may even encourage such individuals to limit their

---

[121] Alan C. Monheit, Joel C. Cantor, Margaret Koller, and Kimberley S. Fox, "Community Rating and Sustainable Individual Health Insurance Markets in New Jersey," *Health Affairs* 23, no. 4, (2004).

working hours.[122] Hence, a projection that the largest decline in labor supply comes from those earning low incomes can be concluded.[123]

With the implementation of the ACA, taxes rose and the burden of taxes did not fall exclusively on the wealthy.[124] Nearly 5.2 million earners with incomes greater than $200,000 now had to pay increased payroll tax in addition to investment income tax.[125] Moreover, fines for the lack of insurance by approximately 3.9 million Americans, in addition to around one million indigent individuals earning less than two times the federal poverty line, were in place.[126]

Another clever means of getting money is to levy a 40 percent surtax on the Cadillac plans.[127] Cadillac plans are the best among the employer-provided healthcare plans. Whether or not the employer pays a surtax, the government reaps the benefits.[128] For instance, if the employer lowers the standard of insurance and compensates the employee by raising their salary, the government can simply collect that increased income tax.[129] The government also took into consideration that some small employers would

---

122 Ibid.
123 Kimberly Amadeo, "What is Obamacare?" *The Balance*, September 17, 2020.
124 Ibid.
125 Kimberly Amadeo, "What is Obamacare?" *The Balance*, September 17, 2020.
126 Ibid.
127 Kimberly Amadeo, "What is Obamacare?" *The Balance*, September 17, 2020.
128 Ibid.
129 Kimberly Amadeo, "What is Obamacare?" *The Balance*, September 17, 2020.

give up employee insurance entirely and compensate employees through higher wages.[130] However, these wages were taxed, unlike the tax-deductible insurance.

This is the end result of believing the concept of taxing the wealthy. The vast majority of society, which includes the indigent individuals and the middle class, must pay for the ACA.[131] Governmental guarantees for health insurance companies were necessary politically in order to suppress resistance of insurance companies that were uncertain about what the effects of these new regulations would be. The government has decided to shift some of the risk associated with new legislations on taxpayers.[132] This was done as otherwise the premiums would skyrocket at a much faster rate and perhaps some insurers would withdraw from the market as a result.[133]

Hence, through easing the burden of the insurance companies, in addition to their clients, the government was now able to look better in the eyes of the public, who were unaware of all of this. In 2014, government subsidies made the premiums 10 percent lower than they otherwise would have been.[134] Consequently, the costs associated with the ACA were concealed from voters.[135]

---

130 Ibid.

131 Kimberly Amadeo, "What is Obamacare?" *The Balance*, September 17, 2020.

132 Ibid.

133 Kimberly Amadeo, "What is Obamacare?" *The Balance*, September 17, 2020.

134 Ibid.

135 Kimberly Amadeo, "What is Obamacare?" *The Balance*, September 17, 2020.

Companies employing at least fifty full-time employees were forced to insure them under penalties between $2,000 and $3,000 per employee.[136]

This distorted the labor market and prevented the development of companies. For instance, if a company wants to employ forty-nine individuals, the company would want to avoid either the necessity of insuring all of them or paying the fine, hence another employee would likely not be hired. In contrast, if a company employs fifty-four individuals, it might be profitable to fire five of those employees. This creates an incentive for small businesses to stay small. In contrast, large companies are encouraged to have a maximum number of part-time employees since the fines are paid for only full-time employees. Between the years of 2015 and 2024, the US government expects employers will pay around $319 billion in these penalties.[137]

In 2009, the typical cost of medical care was around $8,000 per person.[138] In 2014, the cost rose to $9,400.[139] Between 2009 and 2014, the cumulative inflation was around 10.3 percent.[140] When taking inflation into consideration separately, it would be expected that the expenditure should rise only to

---

136 Ibid.
137 Kimberly Amadeo, "What is Obamacare?" *The Balance*, September 17, 2020.
138 Ibid.
139 Kimberly Amadeo, "What is Obamacare?" *The Balance*, September 17, 2020.
140 Ibid.

$8,827 instead of $9,400.[141] Hence, it can be seen that medical expenditures have increased over time.[142] Currently, the expenditures on medical care, when considered in accordance to the GDP, are above 17 percent.[143]

Currently, there is nothing being done to deeply reform the US healthcare system to eliminate the root causes of these astronomical costs. Rather, the government has simply forced more individuals into this ineffective system, and the burden of paying for this system is levied on society.

AN INTERVIEW WITH DAN ROSS—HEALTH ROSETTA

In an interview with Dan Ross, advisor to the Health Rosetta, Dan states that right now, there are two main platforms that exist in healthcare: Medicare Advantage and Humana. Through Medicare Advantage, one signs a contract with CMS for Medicare in return for a monthly risk-adjusted premium. Humana, on the other hand, is a Medicare Advantage company with the potential to improve US healthcare. Dan is a firm believer that free market in healthcare is essential and that we must accept people profiting to ensure people are healthy.

Through the implementation of a primary care model, the provider directs the care and thus provides much more streamlined care. This has been observed to work well in the United Kingdom, Europe, and Central and South America.

---

141 Kimberly Amadeo, "What is Obamacare?" *The Balance*, September 17, 2020.

142 Ibid.

143 Kimberly Amadeo, "What is Obamacare?" *The Balance*, September 17, 2020.

The United States, we currently have a commercial healthcare business with lobbying and corruption inherent in our system. Dan believes using big data would cut healthcare costs to a tenth or maybe even a twentieth of current costs. Moreover, big data would provide a means of increasing transparency in the opaque healthcare system that we have right now. Through this commercial healthcare business, the US healthcare system is inherently disease centric. Profits for companies and shareholders are higher when people are sicker. This is why there are high-deductible plans. Moreover, corruption is evident through hidden money sent to consultants. We are in essence paying for bad performance.

If a scenario where there is the opportunity to reduce inpatient care by, say, 50 percent arises, insurance companies are not going to be pleased, as they would be losing money in this scenario.

Costs vary drastically across the world for the same exact procedure and/or medications. An excellent example of this is observed through Dr. Shetty's practice as an Indian cardiac surgeon. In his practice, bypass surgery costs around $1,600, whereas in the United States it costs about $80,000. Interestingly, outcomes are better in Dr. Shetty's practice, and he does six times as many surgeries as those found in US hospitals. His practice in the Cayman Islands does more free pediatric open-heart surgeries than in every other hospital in the United States combined. This exemplifies the disease-centric US healthcare system.

In order for a solution to be reached, Dan believes a shift toward value-based healthcare is essential. This is not likely to come from the government because they are paid by the healthcare industry executives profiting from the current system. In fact, in the first quarter of 2020, there was enough money sent to Washington, DC, to pay every member of Congress $300,000.[144] Rather, the solution is most likely from the "purchasers of healthcare." Employers must demand value, where value = performance + safety.

CONCLUSION
- The problem with community rating is there is an incorrect underlying assumption that people are identical in health status, and this ends up harming those who actually take care of their own health.

- Currently, there is nothing being done to deeply reform the US healthcare system to eliminate the root causes of these astronomical costs. Rather, the government has simply forced more individuals into this ineffective system, and the burden of paying for this system is levied on society.

- According to Dan Ross, a free market in healthcare is essential. The primary care model is executed well in other regions of the world (United Kingdom, Europe, Central America, and South America), hence it should be explored here in the United States where there is currently a disease-centric profit model in healthcare. The solution is most likely from the "purchasers of healthcare." Employers must demand value, where value = performance + safety. Dan believes this will pave the shift toward a value-based system.

---

144 Ibid.

CHAPTER 3

THE THEORY OF *AUTONOMY*

Ms. Lewis was transferred to the medical intensive care unit (MICU) with liver failure in January under my watch. There was a negative chest X-ray and a positive purified protein derivative screening signifying a tuberculosis diagnosis, as Ms. Lewis was infected with the mycobacterium tuberculosis. Therapy for possible latent tuberculosis infection was initiated. Following several weeks, the patient felt fatigued, had right upper quadrant abdominal pain, and was found to have elevated results from the liver functions test.

When the patient, physician, and I had a conversation regarding Ms. Lewis's condition, I learned three main things.

First, do not assume every patient fits the criteria for a medical condition. After treatment, the patient desired medical care for abdominal pain. However, the patient did not receive the medical care despite being asked if the patient had a reaction to the Isoniazid (INH) antibiotic. Ms. Lewis's symptoms intensified, and she still did not receive proper care. A few days afterward, Ms. Lewis went to the ER and still the international normalized ratio (INR), a type of calculation based on the prothrombin time test to see how well blood clots, was not assessed properly. In fact, Ms. Lewis was regaled by a physician on Prometheus, whose liver was eaten by a crow. In short, the physician dismissed Ms. Lewis's pain as the liver regenerating.

However, after Ms. Lewis's ER visit, she was in the ICU discussing several possibilities including death. Thanks to the gastroenterologist (GI) doctor, Ms. Lewis was able to survive. The GI doctor looked at the laboratory data from the tests ordered, and through this he was able to recognize that Ms. Lewis had liver failure. He then called Ms. Lewis and admitted her to the hospital.

Second, the patient is at first a person. Likewise, every physician is also a person. A matter of importance is that the underlying inherent trait is humanity. Throughout this ongoing battle Ms. Lewis underwent, there were several medical workers who disrespected her in the process of communication and her care. It is important to recognize that the only person living through the long-term physical ramifications in terms of the disease is the patient. Ignorance is a very common occurrence. Per Ms. Lewis, there was a physician who assessed her of being an alcoholic to hide her mistakes. This was an unfounded conclusion.

Nurse Mary was in charge of bathing Ms. Lewis. She was quintessential to the restoration of Ms. Lewis's faith in humanity, in addition to the profession of medicine. Nurse Mary spoke to her, looking into her eyes and allowing her to maintain her dignity. In short, she allowed Ms. Lewis to be treated as a healthy human should be treated.

Another time, Ms. Lewis recalled a resident visiting her and speaking of his medical adventures.

One particularly eye-catching story for Ms. Lewis was of a resident's encounter with a patient put on salt water for IV drip. The interesting situation was that the patient had quite a large dysfunctional family who were not willing to speak with each other. Moreover, each individual member of this patient's family wanted to hear from medical personnel separately as they argued that they were entitled to hear from medical personnel. The discussion revolved around why salt water was used in lieu of Gatorade. Ms. Lewis recalls the resident conveying that the son argued at one point that Gatorade should be given because it is more isotonic. Then the resident explained that salt water has more electrolytes than Gatorade does. Such questions continued for over an hour and spanned across the entire patient's family present at the hospital.

This act of the resident sharing his experience enabled the patient, Ms. Lewis, to be more at ease and more open with the resident. As such, these experiences highlight the human aspect of medicine that is imperative and that we possess as patients and as physicians.

Finally, one should never assume the patient is the perpetrator of their condition and should not treat them as if they were. Ms. Lewis recalls some of the stigma associated with her condition. She recalls Nurse Britney, while performing a blood draw, saying, "You really have been enjoying life," in reference to her to being an alcoholic. Without questioning whether or not Ms. Lewis was necessarily responsible for her condition, the nurse made assumptions. This premature formation of opinion is harmful.

In contrast to Nurse Britney's nonprofessionalism, Ms. Lewis appreciated and praised her team of doctors for lifting her spirits. Medical doctors practice in the hope of doing no harm, first and foremost. As a patient, Ms. Lewis states, "The few bad apples really leave a bitter taste."

As a future physician myself, it is empowering for me to trust patients and to not have blind faith in the current state of medicine. Medicine is constantly evolving; there is always room for improvement.

Had the medical team served Ms. Lewis justice, she would not have been put on a medication that caused her liver to fail despite having the classic textbook symptoms.

UNDERSTANDING *AUTONOMY*

Generally, there are invoked capacities of self-governance. In bioethics, however, autonomy refers to personal rule of oneself based on adequate information without influences on those choices.[145]

As an autonomous actor, you act with intention, have an adequate understanding of your role, and are free of influence by others.

The current standard for autonomy in bioethics shows providers do not apply this standard of autonomy to children, those incapacitated, or those who may be in a position to

---

145 Jukka Varelius, "The value of autonomy in medical ethics," *Medicine, Health Care, and Philosophy* 9, no. 3 (December 2006).

be exploited by others.[146] There is an undeniable need for intervention for patients who have varying degrees of nonautonomous characteristics above a certain threshold.

On this note, a major issue of medical paternalism arises.

To understand paternalism, I will present analogies. Consider the treatment of patients as a benevolent father would treat his child. Also, consider a benevolent, paternal governmental system. These analogies are based on the premise that the government and the father are obliged to be beneficiary toward those they protect.

Within healthcare, these analogies serve as the root of the idea that medical providers have the training and the expertise to be in a position of authority to best serve those in their care. This is the basis for the various laws and regulations that fall under this paternalistic principle.

To start, I will explore the following question.

> *Would you support strong paternalism whereby providers protect certain patients from significant risks despite limitations on their will?*

Let us say a patient requests to leave the hospital, but you as the provider know death is a very likely outcome. Would you let the patient leave? I advise you to approach this question from a nonlegal perspective. This is a purely moral question.

---

146 Ibid.

If one were to consider decision making the only facet of autonomy, many other manifestations are neglected from consideration. This is why it is important to decentralize autonomy. In this light, the ability to plan and perform actions are important considerations.

Currently, the working assumption is patients have autonomy if they show the ability to be able to make informed decisions. Healthcare workers are obligated to ensure this capacity does not decline, whether this be by disease or other factors. When patients are deemed to have autonomy, they are deemed competent to make decisions. It is thereby the duty of healthcare providers to respect their decisions and abide by them.

CONCLUSION
- 3 Important lessons I learned from Ms. Lewis:

    - Do not assume every patient fits the criteria for a medical condition.

    - The patient is at first a person. Likewise, every physician is also a person. A matter of importance is that the underlying inherent trait is humanity.

    - One should never assume the patient is the perpetrator of their condition and should not treat them as if they were.

- Autonomy refers to personal rule of oneself based on adequate information without influences on those choices.

CHAPTER 4

A MULTIDIMENSIONAL APPROACH TO PATIENT AUTONOMY

———

Here, I present a multidimensional approach to patient autonomy covering executive, narrative, informative, functional, and decisional autonomy.[147] The first step in patient autonomy advocacy is to identify the specific autonomy affected. These autonomy manifestations are not mutually exclusive, nor are they necessarily dependent. Through an interpretative phenomenological analysis, it is evident that when one's autonomy dimension is hindered, it disrupts their identity.

One of the major consequences of suboptimal patient autonomy is manifested in poor treatment adherence, especially in chronic illness. This is because, for chronic ailments, adherence is viewed as how much overlap there

---

147 Jukka Varelius, "The value of autonomy in medical ethics," *Medicine, Health Care, and Philosophy* 9, no. 3 (December 2006).

is between a medical provider's recommendations and the behavior of the patient. This can be observed in the case of psoriasis, which is a chronic dermatological condition that has a poor adherence rate. In fact, in Spain, 85 percent of patients who are diagnosed with psoriasis do not adhere to their treatment.[148]

In the fifth edition of *Principles of Biomedical Ethics*, Beauchamp and Childress propose that all autonomy theories are based on two premises: agency and liberty.[149] Liberty refers to the ability to not be under the influence of any restraint.[150] Agency refers to the ability to make decisions with intent.[151] Current clinical literature is heavily focused on protecting patients' rights; however, there is very little focus on the subjective attributes of patient autonomy.

The definitions of autonomy were initially designed for healthy individuals, not those with illness.[152] Moreover, the concepts of autonomy are focused on acute care, not on chronic care.[153] As such, the focus is on decisional autonomy. Thus, the tendency is to conclude that autonomous decision making is identical to patient autonomy.

---

148 Ibid.
149 James F. Childress and Tom L. Beauchamp. *Principles of Biomedical Ethics 5th Edition* (Oxford: Oxford University Press, 2001).
150 Ibid.
151 James F. Childress and Tom L. Beauchamp. *Principles of Biomedical Ethics 5th Edition* (Oxford: Oxford University Press, 2001).
152 Jukka Varelius, "The value of autonomy in medical ethics," *Medicine, Health Care, and Philosophy* 9, no. 3 (December 2006).
153 Ibid.

Addressing chronic disease treatment is imperative to societies that have an increasingly aging population. Not adhering to medical treatment has dire consequences, such as exorbitant costs of a healthcare system since there are higher levels of patient admission to a hospital, less disease control, social attrition, and overarchingly a lower quality of life.

The adherence rates in developed countries such as the United States are around 50 percent and are even lower in the case of developing countries.[154]

In recent years, approaches for patient adherence to medical treatment for chronic ailments have undergone several modifications. Originally, the view was that the patient is not compliant, which is when a patient adheres to the treatment as ascribed by the medical provider.[155] Compliance is now viewed as a passive behavior by a patient. Due to this change of thought, adherence is the preferred alternative to the implied active patient participation in their medical care. Adherence accounts for both the behavior of the patient and the environment of the patient. With this broad range of factors within adherence, medical providers can contribute to the poor adherence of medical care by patients through a poor consideration of a patient's environment or by having a poor doctor–patient relationship.

---

154 Jukka Varelius, "The value of autonomy in medical ethics," *Medicine, Health Care, and Philosophy* 9, no. 3 (December 2006).

155 Ibid.

THE PSORIASIS MODEL

Psoriasis is characterized by skin and occasional joint inflammation.[156] The cause is abnormally rapid skin cell renewal.[157] For the healthy person, skin cells are typically repaired at a rate of every month.[158] In contrast, for psoriasis patients, this skin cell repair process takes less than a week.[159] Importantly, psoriasis is a chronic disease and, as a result, is an excellent disease model to study when discussing patient autonomy.[160]

PATIENT AUTONOMY DIMENSIONS

Due to prevailing clinical literature reducing patient autonomy to the mere ability to make decisions, the current view is that patient autonomy has been reached when patients show the ability to make informed decisions.[161]

Decisional autonomy is defined as the capability to consider and then act on that consideration.[162] There are three requirements to fulfill this definition: (1) no external duress

---

156 Adriana Rendon and Knut Schakel, "Psoriasis Pathogenesis and Treatment," *International Journal of Molecular Sciences* 20, no. 6 (March 2019).

157 Ibid.

158 Adriana Rendon and Knut Schakel, "Psoriasis Pathogenesis and Treatment," *International Journal of Molecular Sciences* 20, no. 6 (March 2019).

159 Ibid.

160 Adriana Rendon and Knut Schakel, "Psoriasis Pathogenesis and Treatment," *International Journal of Molecular Sciences* 20, no. 6 (March 2019).

161 Jukka Varelius, "The Value of Autonomy in Medical Ethics," *Medicine, Health Care, and Philosophy* 9, no. 3 (December 2006).

162 Ibid.

or coercion, (2) enough information is given in order for one to make a reasoned decision, and (3) having the cognitive ability to make an informed decision.[163]

Decisional autonomy is not just constrained to informed consent. By reducing autonomy in this way, the work of medical providers is often hampered and generates a culture of mistrust among the different members who are involved in the care of the patient. The subjective aspects of care are neglected, and the consequence is that patients are forced to make decisions, yet their autonomy is dismissed.

In the context of chronic care, the individualist view on bioethical discourse is not fitting. As a result, it is important to contextualize patient autonomy for each patient based on their individualized physiological and psychological conditions.

Work carried out on dependence has proven that it is important to differentiate the ability of decision making from the process of decision making.

There are several measures that look at the functional capability of decision making, including the Convention on the Rights of Persons with Disabilities (CRPD).[164]

However, the issue with these classifications is their inherently arbitrary nature. The current evaluation standard is *statistical norm*, according to the World Health Organization

---

163 Jukka Varelius, "The Value of Autonomy in Medical Ethics," *Medicine, Health Care, and Philosophy* 9, no. 3 (December 2006).

164 Ibid.

(WHO).[165] However, it is very difficult to establish statistical norm for every human activity. For instance, the CRPD divides human disability into four categories: mental, intellectual, sensory, and physical impairments.[166] Whereas, the ICF divides human functionality into eight categories: voice and speech; sensory, pain, and mental; metabolic; cardiothoracic; genitourinary; skeletal; integumentary; and related.[167]

Some may propose that the difference is simply that ICF is more detailed in its categorization. This is indeed the case; however, the methodology of classification is the issue here. More specifically, CRPD differentiates between intellectual and mental capacity, yet ICF includes intellectual capacity within mental capacity.[168]

Functional autonomy is based on physiological functionality.[169] It is the joint contribution of both physiological functional capacity and execution that defines functional autonomy.[170] Thus, the individual and the environment are interdependent into what comprises a lack of functional autonomy.

However, when discussing a chronic disease, patient autonomy increases but also increases in complexity. Autonomy now

---

165 Jukka Varelius, "The Value of Autonomy in Medical Ethics," *Medicine, Health Care, and Philosophy* 9, no. 3 (December 2006).

166 Ibid.

167 Jukka Varelius, "The Value of Autonomy in Medical Ethics," *Medicine, Health Care, and Philosophy* 9, no. 3 (December 2006).

168 Ibid.

169 Jukka Varelius, "The Value of Autonomy in Medical Ethics," *Medicine, Health Care, and Philosophy* 9, no. 3 (December 2006).

170 Ibid.

becomes an extended process. *Executive autonomy* can be defined as the ability to make decisions and adhere to them over time.[171]

Medical providers generally interpret the incompliance of patients as an autonomous refusal. However, this is not always the case—especially for patients with chronic conditions who may find themselves not being able to perform the prescribed treatment on a consistent basis. This is of ethical concern as a result.

Through *narrative medicine*, there can be a greater emphasis on seeing beyond the symptoms and being more encompassing of the environmental influences.[172] This can be a means of increasing rates of executive autonomy.

Narrative autonomy is the ability of patients to understand and communicate that understanding for effective therapeutic intervention.[173]

Lastly, *informative autonomy* refers to the ability of patients to access information—both public and private.[174] The information is of intrinsic value to allow for the patient to make their own decisions and also to decide in what capacity they will be sharing the information with others.

---

171 Jukka Varelius, The Value of Autonomy in Medical Ethics," *Medicine, Health Care, and Philosophy* 9, no. 3 (December 2006).

172 Ibid.

173 Jukka Varelius, "The Value of Autonomy in Medical Ethics," *Medicine, Health Care, and Philosophy* 9, no. 3 (December 2006).

174 Ibid.

HOW AUTONOMIES RELATE

When considering the legal constructs of autonomy, many equate *autonomy* with a psychological capability that individuals have to make decisions. Thus, the underlying premise here is *mental state*.[175] Other features, whether intrinsic or extrinsic, are built from this foundational premise. This approach clearly does not work in the medical field because there are so many variances in the autonomy of patients.

Therefore, it is imperative to view patient autonomy as an amalgamation of the five autonomies. Analogously, the five autonomies can be viewed as a row of dominos. If any one of the autonomies is impaired, the other four autonomies are detrimentally affected as a result. Thus, the ideal means of approaching patient autonomy is by considering them independently but also seeing the psychological-social-biological interconnecting thread.

In the psychiatric unit, there are many patients who have an impaired narrative autonomy, yet many are able to make uncomplicated decisions. However, since their decisional autonomy is working, this form of autonomy is incoherent since the narrative itself is unformed.

An individual who has suffered an occupational accident lacks autonomy despite normal psychological ability for decision making. The opposite case, where an individual presents a mental disorder but has normal physical ability, still lacks autonomy. The first case has functional autonomy impairment.

---

175   Jukka Varelius, "The Value of Autonomy in Medical Ethics," *Medicine, Health Care, and Philosophy* 9, no. 3 (December 2006).

The second case has decisional autonomy impairment. Thus, it is evident that an individual's mental capacity rests at the intersection of both functional and decisional autonomy.

However, this interconnecting line is not limited to functional and decisional autonomy; it applies to all areas of human autonomy. Mental capacity is fundamental to autonomy; however, it is not all-encompassing to enable autonomy to be achieved in the medical setting.

This can be elucidated through the example of psoriasis, which has several variances. Individuals who have been diagnosed with psoriasis are able to perform everyday activities, however, adherence is of concern here.[176] Now, I will explain how adherence to treatment for patients with chronic conditions can be increased by examining the intersection of executive and decisional autonomy.

INCREASING CHRONIC TREATMENT ADHERENCE— EXECUTIVE & DECISIONAL AUTONOMY

Currently, the MacArthur Competence Assessment Tool for Treatment (MacCAT-T) is viewed as the gold standard for studying mental competence.[177] This tool evaluates four different areas: choice expression, comprehension of relevant information, proper assessment, and logical reasoning.[178]

---

176 Adriana Rendon and Knut Schakel, "Psoriasis Pathogenesis and Treatment," *International Journal of Molecular Sciences* Vol. 20 no. 6, March 2019.

177 T. Grisso, P. S. Appelbaum, and C. Hill-Fotouhi, "The MacCAT-T: a clinical tool to assess patients' capacities to make treatment decisions," *Psychiatric Services* 48, no. 11, (November 1997).

178 Ibid.

Personally, I believe adherence is a missing evaluation area that would really strengthen this tool. Executive capability partly has a biological component. This is especially relevant in fields such as neurology and psychiatry.

The neurological basis of executive functions is found in the *frontal lobe* of the brain. From studies on the relationship between executive function impairments and chronic care outcomes, critical empirical evidence has shown that it is important to access the ability to make a decision and to focus specifically on the self-management care ability.[179]

There are several medical examinations that study various facets of executive functionality. The Wisconsin Card Sorting Test (WCST) is the most commonly used.[180] The only significant downside to using WCST is the complexity.[181] Due to this, there have been more recent tests that are far simpler to use. One of these tests is called the Frontal Behavioral Inventory survey, which looks at the changes, both negative and positive, in a patient's behavior.[182] These changes are believed to be

---

179 Patricia A. Grady and Lisa Lucio Gough,"Self-Management: A Comprehensive Approach to Management of Chronic Conditions," *American Journal of Public Health* 14, no. 8, (August 2014).

180 A. Campana, F. Macciardi, O. Gambini, and S. Scarone, "The Wisconsin Card Sorting Test (WCST) performance in normal subjects: a twin study," *Neuropsychobiology* 14, no. 7, (1996).

181 Ibid.

182 A. Kertesz, N. Nadkarni, W. Davidson, and A. W. Thomas, "The Frontal Behavioral Inventory in the differential diagnosis of frontotemporal dementia," *Journal of the International Neuropsychological Society* 6, no. 4, (May 2000).

reflective of changes happening on a physiological level in the prefrontal region of the frontal lobe.[183]

One of the ways in which executive functionality can be better studied is by expanding the MacCAT-T with other examinations to obtain a more encompassing tool.[184] More specifically, the MacCAT-T examining reasoning, understanding, choice preference, and appreciation should be supplemented with psychobehavioral analysis of the executive functionality.[185]

When considering consistent patient revisits due to some marker of not adhering to medical advice, the medical provider might wish to examine the possibility of the *executive autonomy* being compromised. This may or may not involve other forms of autonomy, such as *decisional autonomy*. Therefore, to plan effective therapeutic intervention, it is important to look at the intersection of executive functionality and decisional functionality impairments. These impairments can be offset through adequate social and clinical support.

Importantly, a poor level of executive autonomy does not necessarily mean the root cause is impairment; rather, it may be indicative of some common condition. In fact, even as a healthy being, one may lack the strength to adhere to their prescribed route to achieve their goal. The only difference for medically ill individuals is that this lack of strength now steers toward treatment adherence.

---

183 Ibid.

184 T. Grisso, P. S. Appelbaum, and C. Hill-Fotouhi, "The MacCAT-T: a clinical tool to assess patients' capacities to make treatment decisions," *Psychiatric Services* 48, no. 11, (November 1997).

185 Ibid.

Going back to times of Classical Greece in the fourth and fifth centuries BC, most of the ethical constructs were rooted in *akrasia*, which is the state of mind where one has a weak will and so acts against what is in their best interest.[186] Simply put, it is a lack of self-control. In the seventh book of Aristotle's *Nicomachean Ethics*, some of the most prevalent cases of variance-ridden morality division were observed.[187] The idea was that when rationality wins, you get *enkrateia*, which means you have self-control.[188] However, when irrationality wins, you get *akrasia*.[189]

Moreover, just as functional diversity exists, so does executive diversity. This is due to both the pathological variances as well as environmental ones.

As such, by steering what defines adherence on an individualistic level that examines one's unique pathological and environmental variances, excellent outcomes are more likely—especially in the case of chronic diseases such as psoriasis.

IDENTITY–AUTONOMY OVERLAP

Viewing patient autonomy from a social construct perspective, this viewpoint is exemplified by the feminist perspective.

---

186 Aristotle. *Nicomachean Ethics Book VII: Symposium Aristotelicum*. Oxford: Oxford University Press, 2005.

187 Ibid.

188 Aristotle. *Nicomachean Ethics Book VII: Symposium Aristotelicum*. Oxford: Oxford University Press, 2005.

189 Ibid.

In the mid-1970s, feminism was strongly in favor of the potential of autonomy in promoting increased rights and privileges for women.[190] However, in the 1980s, this view was the opposite—firm opposition on autonomy.[191] The view was that an individual would be viewed as an isolated being and not be encompassing of other environmental influences.[192] Yet, in the 1990s, there was once again an interest in autonomy, more pertinently with regard to *relational autonomy*, which is encompassing of other environmental influences such as the social determinants of health—social status, gender, and race.[193]

Thus, relational autonomy puts the ability to do something within the context of one's environment.[194]

Within medicine, the current view of autonomy is well-fitted for the healthy, and thus the definition is restricted to the domains of psychological and behavioral abilities. This is restricting for chronic care.

Inter alia, there is a need for the intersection of neurobiological and relational autonomy viewpoints. The human brain has the ability to organize cognitive thought; however, these decisions are far from independent of environmental impact.

---

190 Jukka Varelius, "The value of autonomy in medical ethics," *Medicine, Health Care, and Philosophy* 9, no. 3, (December 2006).

191 Ibid.

192 Jukka Varelius, "The value of autonomy in medical ethics," *Medicine, Health Care, and Philosophy* 9, no. 3, (December 2006).

193 Ibid.

194 Jukka Varelius, "The value of autonomy in medical ethics," *Medicine, Health Care, and Philosophy* 9, no. 3, (December 2006).

Functional, decisional, and executive autonomies can be viewed as *constitutive* since they are intrinsic. In contrast, informative and narrative autonomies are interactive due to their reliance on both neurobiological and environmental factors.

Ethical judgements are based on *intrinsic* and *extrinsic* factors. This means that a patient's autonomy is due to the perception that an individual has of themselves as a patient based on their extrinsic interactions with others who are involved in both their medical and social care during the illness-care process. As a result, human illness can no longer be viewed as merely an illness. This is one of the negatives of evidence-based medicine. The prioritization of disease over patient is contributing to a decline in quality of care.

The medical care relationship between a medical provider and a patient is initiated with an illness—more specifically, the suffering that is associated with the illness. When an individual is ill, there is a deviance between one's perception of themselves and others' perception of them. This deviance among the perceptions implies a maladjusted *narrative autonomy*. Seen in the case of psoriasis, this visible dermatological condition is a prime reason for why there is such a low adherence to medical treatment as advised by a provider. In order to properly address low adherence rates in chronic conditions, it is important to examine the *executive autonomy* and provide treatment based on this information.

CONCLUSION

- Liberty refers to the ability to not be under the influence of any restraint. Agency refers to the ability to make decisions with intent.

- Compliance is now viewed as a passive behavior by a patient. Due to this change of thought, adherence is the preferred alternative to the implied active patient participation in their medical care.

- Psoriasis is a chronic disease and, as a result, is an excellent disease model to study when discussing patient autonomy.

- *Decisional autonomy* is where patients have the ability to decide on a particular action from several plausible choices.

- *Functional autonomy* relates to one's control of their physical, sensory, and mental state.

- *Executive autonomy* is the capacity to carry out a particular decision and have the ability to maintain that particular decision.

- *Narrative autonomy* is the capacity patients have to be able to understand the circumstances of their present condition.

- *Informative autonomy* is the ability to control and access information that is public, private, and personal. This may be manifested when a patient decides for themselves to disclose information in regard to their health.

- The underlying premise of autonomy is *mental state.*

- By steering what defines adherence on an individualistic level that examines one's unique pathological and environmental variances, excellent outcomes are more likely—especially in the case of chronic diseases such as psoriasis.

- Functional, decisional, and executive autonomies can be viewed as *constitutive* since they are intrinsic. In contrast, informative and narrative autonomies are interactive due to their reliance on both neurobiological and environmental factors.

- In order to properly address low adherence rates in chronic conditions, it is important to examine the *executive autonomy* and provide treatment based on this information.

CHAPTER 5

CASE STUDY— PATIENT AUTONOMY

———

While witnessing her husband die, a sixty-year-old woman, Claire, wrote a living will in the ICU. She instructed all medical practitioners involved in potential medical care that under no circumstances were they to apply resuscitation. In a document that was signed, dated, and seen by a lawyer, she wrote, "DO NOT TAKE ME TO THIS HOSPITAL." A copy of this letter was given to her general practitioner (GP).

Later, she developed a malignant melanoma. However, rather than seek medical advice, she kept the matter a secret until the lesion was observed by a family member. Medical advice was then reluctantly sought, but she declined any sort of excision or biopsy for several weeks until the lesion was very obvious and local lymphadenopathy, swollen lymph nodes, had developed. Finally she agreed to cosmetic surgery and a biopsy, although it was explained to her that, by this time, this could only be palliative, to improve the quality of life. Over the next few weeks, she had several consultations with her

GP, and the situation and her prognosis were discussed very openly on each occasion. She requested euthanasia from her GP more than once. This was refused, but the GP promised to honor her wishes and provide the best possible palliative care.

She became weaker but declined all offers of help and support from her family, district nurses, and MacMillan nurses. However, one morning she collapsed and suffered an epileptic fit. Much against her will, her elderly but fit parents (aged eighty-one and eighty-three years) moved in to care for her. An outpatient computerized tomography (CT) scan and magnetic resonance imaging (MRI) scan confirmed cerebral as well as hepatic metastases, tumors originating outside of the central nervous system comprised of the brain and the spinal cord and spread to the central nervous system via blood systems.

Several weeks elapsed during which the patient became weaker yet retained full mental capacity. The GP visited regularly and on each occasion was asked by the patient how long it was likely to be before she died. This was invariably answered by explaining there was no way of knowing the exact details or timings. Repeated attempts were made to explain the possibility of further convulsions as a terminal event, but the patient was extremely reluctant to consider the mode of her death. She simply reiterated her desire to die as soon as possible and her absolute wish not to go to the local hospital.

Things changed dramatically one afternoon, only two hours after a routine house call by the GP, when she developed a further epileptic fit. Even though afternoon surgery was about to start, the GP attended immediately. The patient was in the throes of a generalized tonic-clonic convulsion, involving of loss of consciousness and violent muscle contractions, and her parents, not surprisingly, were in a state of acute distress. The doctor administered ten milligrams of rectal diazepam to treat seizures, but this failed to arrest the convulsion. Due to her express wishes, which had been made so abundantly clear, an ambulance was not called initially.

However, after thirty minutes and with no sign of the convulsion ceasing, an emergency call was put in. Because of the remote location of the patient's home and certain staffing issues among other professionals such as district nursing and palliative care colleagues, it was not possible to obtain further supplies of diazepam until the ambulance arrived after a long delay. This meant that the patient had been in status epilepticus, a seizure lasting for at least thirty minutes, for more than two hours by the time a further ten milligrams of diazepam were given intravenously and an oxygen mask was applied by the paramedics. The patient became sedated although low-level fitting continued.

Local protocol dictated that any 911 call should be taken to the nearest hospital, in this case the same hospital the patient had so expressly stated she would not be taken to. A further ninety minutes were taken in telephone calls to managers in local hospitals, the ambulance service, district nursing service, palliative care professionals, and others before permission was eventually granted for the patient to be taken to a hospital approximately twenty-five miles away, normally considered "out of area." She spent that night in the emergency (A&E) department before being transferred to a ward later the next day. She died a week later without regaining consciousness.

Cases like this are clearly rare, but the new Mental Capacity Act demands we respect our patients' autonomy (particularly in respect to advanced decisions) and act in their best interests in the case of incapacity.

The patient had made it clear in written form she did not want to be resuscitated nor to be admitted to the local hospital. However, she had been reluctant to discuss her mode of death. For the GP to act in the patient's best interests, the primary concern was to stop the convulsions, even if hospital admission was required. How many GPs would have been happy to leave a patient fitting at home in the presence of her elderly distressed parents? Is there a point at which the duty of care to a patient who is unconscious is superseded by the duty of care to others, in this case the elderly parents? Should there be a "get-out clause" in advanced decisions for exceptional cases where distress to others may outweigh the need to respect the patient's wishes?

> *How does a doctor balance duty of care to one patient who will die very soon against the duty of care to other patients? In this case, an entire afternoon was taken with this scenario and the doctor's evening surgery had to be taken by another doctor. The GP in this case is usually singlehanded. If the other doctor had not been available, what would have happened to all the other patients seeking medical attention that afternoon? Is it right for them to suffer while the GP is involved in one particularly complicated case?*

The move toward patient autonomy and against "doctor knows best" is undoubtedly a positive one. The Mental Capacity Act of 2005 clarifies many of the points already present under common law.[195] In interpreting the act, we must be aware that in not all cases will it be clear that respecting patients' decisions and acting in their best interests are the same thing, and in this case, patient autonomy is the primary concern. However, we should also remember physicians are a rationed resource which needs to be shared with all patients.

---

195 "Mental Capacity Act," *NHS*, 27 January, 2021.

CHAPTER 6

HEALTH SYSTEM IN FLUX

―――

CURRENT STATE OF AFFAIRS

It was early March 2020, and the COVID-19 pandemic had begun to exert significant effects across much of the world. As the project lead for the Coronavirus Visualization Team based at Harvard University, I was responsible for the creation of a geospatial dashboard that looked at various factors before and after the COVID-19 pandemic. Our team looked at factors such as how many deaths, on average, occurred in each of the fifty states; internet usage; and crime rates. The goal was that these factors visually displayed on a geospatial dashboard would enable researchers, policymakers, and the general public alike to visually understand how COVID-19 was affecting our community.

Here, I present the data with regard to COVID-19 impacts and some policy resolutions, some of which I presented at the 2020 CollatEd Ministerial Global Governance Summit.

The COVID-19 pandemic has brought into attention, now more than ever before, the need for healthcare reform, particularly in regard to accessibility. Although virtually all aspects of United States healthcare are facing incredible challenges throughout this pandemic, the macedoine manner in which pay and regulation of healthcare are unraveling during this time of crisis and urgency is leaving millions vulnerable and showing the need for prompt, well-planned political action to ensure access to affordable healthcare.

Currently, nearly half of Americans receive healthcare through their employers.[196] Now, with record-high numbers of Americans filing for unemployment insurance, millions will find themselves without healthcare insurance in the largest pandemic in a century.[197] Those who are able to maintain insurance coverage may find the care unaffordable now.

According to an *LA Times* survey of adults with employer-sponsored health insurance by Hamel and Brodie with the Kaiser Family Foundation, more than 50 percent of Americans with employer-sponsored health insurance received delayed treatment for either themselves or for a loved one in 2019 due to unaffordability.[198] The pandemic has cost many Americans their career, accompanied income, and health insurance, which will serve to only exacerbate the current healthcare challenges that exist for all Americans. In March

---

196 "How Many Americans Get Health Insurance from their Employer?" *eHealth*, January 11, 2021.

197 Ibid.

198 Liz Hamel, Cailey Munana, and Mollyann Brodie, "Kaiser Family Foundation/LA Times Survey of Adults With Employer-Sponsored Insurance," *KFF*, May 02, 2019.

2020, the Commonwealth Fund issued a poll on the views of Americans on the COVID-19 pandemic.[199] Per that poll, nearly 68 percent of adults stated that out-of-pocket costs they could have to pay would be "somewhat" or "very" important in their decision-making process of whether they would seek care if they had COVID-19 symptoms.[200]

This is a health hazard. When one does not receive care, both in terms of treatment *and* testing, it poses a risk to all those around them by prolonging the pandemic, contributing to higher morbidity and mortality levels and collectively exacerbating the economic impacts.

HEALTHCARE LEGISLATION FOR PANDEMIC CARE

In an effort to address the myriad issues raised by COVID-19, Congress passed two significant pieces of legislation. The Families First Coronavirus Response Act (FFCRA) mandates all private insurers, Medicaid, Medicare, and Medicare Advantage cover COVID-19 testing costs and moreover eliminate cost sharing (coinsurance, copayments, and deductibles) associated with testing services during this time.[201] Congress also appropriated nearly $1 billion for the Public Health and Social Services Emergency Fund to cover COVID-19 testing costs for individuals who are uninsured through

---

199 Ibid.

200 Liz Hamel, Cailey Munana, and Mollyann Brodie, "Kaiser Family Foundation/LA Times Survey of Adults With Employer-Sponsored Insurance," *KFF*, May 02, 2019.

201 "Families First Coronavirus Response Act: Employee Paid Leave Rights," *Wage and Hour Dvision. US Department of Labor.*

their state's Medicaid plans.[202] Patients are susceptible to fees that are involved with the process of cost-sharing fees in hospitalization until their out-of-pocket max per annum is reached—which can exceed $8,000 for an individual and $16,000 for a family.[203]

The Coronavirus Aid, Relief, and Economic Security (CARES) Act passed by Congress is a $2.2 trillion pandemic relief bill mandating that all private plans cover the costs of COVID-19 testing and those associated with future vaccinations.[204] However, the CARES Act falls short of eliminating the cost sharing of COVID-19 symptomatic treatments, such as ventilation and antiviral medications. Regardless, private insurers such as UnitedHealth Group and BlueCross BlueShield have agreed to waive the cost-sharing payments for plan members that are treated for COVID-19.[205] Moreover, the CARES Act has appropriated $100 billion for healthcare providers and hospitals, which Alex Azar, the health and human services secretary, later conditioned on the agreements of providers to not bill insured patients more than their in-network cost-sharing amounts and also to not bill uninsured patients

---

202 "COVID-19 Claims Reimbursement to Health Care Providers and Facilities for Testing, Treatment, and Vaccine Administration for the Uninsured," *Health Resources & Services Administration.*

203 Karyn Schwartz, Karan Pollitz, Jennifer Tolbert, and MayBeth Musumeci, "Gaps in Cost Sharing Protections for COVID-19 Testing and Treatment Could Spark Public Concerns About COVID-19 Vaccine Costs," *KFF*, December 18, 2020.

204 Kellie Moss, Adam Wexler, Lindsey Dawson, Michelle Long, Jennifer Kates, and Juliette Cubanski, "The Coronavirus Aid, Relief, and Economic Security Act: Summary of Key Health Provisions," *KFF*, April 09, 2020.

205 Ibid.

entirely for COVID-19 treatment.[206] In addition, the CARES Act provided emergency grants, loans, and sizable tax credits to assist businesses on either furlough or payroll through June 2020 while extending unemployment benefits for those who lost their jobs.[207]

Through the medium of these laws providing much-needed assistance for many, additional policies are essential to ensure that Americans have continued access to affordable healthcare as the COVID-19 pandemic continues to exert its impacts. Personally, I believe there are several measures that would be prudent to undertake as this pandemic rampages throughout the world. First, policymakers should freeze the insurance status in order to ensure that a maximum number of people are on their existing plan alongside their current providers. Hence, people who had an Affordable Care Act (ACA) marketplace plan or were on employer-sponsored health insurance would be able to remain on that plan through the end of the COVID-19 emergency—even if they are unable to pay their premiums.

On that note, as per data from the Kaiser Family Foundation, there have been various states that have instituted grace periods on paying premiums for all policies.[208] In fact, a

---

206 Kellie Moss, Adam Wexler, Lindsey Dawson, Michelle Long, Jennifer Kates, and Juliette Cubanski, "The Coronavirus Aid, Relief, and Economic Security Act: Summary of Key Health Provisions," *KFF*, April 09, 2020.

207 Ibid.

208 Jennifer Tolbert, Maria Diaz, Cornelia Hall, and Salem Mengistu, "State Actions to Improve the Affordability of Health Insurance in the Individual Market," *KFF*, July 17, 2019.

news release from the office of Ohio Governor Mike DeWine shows that the Ohio Department of Insurance mandated that all insurers offer employers a sixty-day grace period for premium payments in order to allow for employers to retain their employees and consequently their associated health benefits.[209] The federal disaster relief funds would allow for the premium payments to be directly paid, subsidized, or paused.

Second, policymakers ought to expand access to ACA marketplace plans alongside Medicaid to secure coverage for individuals who have lost their jobs. Data from the Kaiser Family Foundation shows that new open enrollment periods for the state ACA marketplaces have been opened in an effort to encourage enrollment in eleven states and the District of Columbia.[210]

According to the Kaiser Family Foundation, data shows that nearly all states received Section 1135 Medicaid waivers in order to meet the needs of their vulnerable residents.[211] There were several states who sought to acquire such waivers for the purpose of waiving preauthorization requirements for COVID-19 related services, eliminating COVID-19-related cost sharing, and facilitating participant–provider enrollment.[212] Additionally, several states paused disenrollment to

---

209 Ibid.

210 Jennifer Tolbert, Maria Diaz, Cornelia Hall, and Salem Mengistu, "State Actions to Improve the Affordability of Health Insurance in the Individual Market," *KFF*, July 17, 2019.

211 Ibid.

212 Jennifer Tolbert, Maria Diaz, Cornelia Hall, and Salem Mengistu, "State Actions to Improve the Affordability of Health Insurance in the Individual Market," *KFF*, July 17, 2019.

receive the higher federal matching rate that was established by the FFCRA.[213] Currently, there is no state enforcing work requirements for maintaining Medicaid eligibility.[214]

Insights from the Kaiser Commission on Medicaid and the Uninsured in collaboration with the United Hospital Fund show that something analogous to a Disease Relief Medicaid (DRM) program could be implemented by government officials. Following September 11, 2001, the DRM allowed for approximately 350,000 New Yorkers to rapidly obtain access to Medicaid benefits by using short-form applications, raising eligibility requirements, and excluding tests for assets.[215] DRM allowed New Yorkers a four-month coverage during the most critical time period of the crisis and also allowed New Yorkers to transition to other coverage.[216] Implementing a similar emergency program could assist people who have lost their jobs or are uninsured during the pandemic by increasing federal matching funds and raising the eligibility criteria beyond Medicaid expansion levels.[217]

Lastly, federal and state officials should continue to address out-of-pocket expenses such as surprise medical billing and cost sharing. According to the American College of Anesthesiologists, surprise medical billing, also known as out-of-network billing, occurs when a patient receives a medical bill for

---

213 Ibid.

214 Jennifer Tolbert, Maria Diaz, Cornelia Hall, and Salem Mengistu, "State Actions to Improve the Affordability of Health Insurance in the Individual Market," *KFF*, July 17, 2019.

215 Ibid.

216 "Surprise Medical Bills/ Out-of-Network Payment," *American Society of Anesthesiologists*.

217 "Cost Sharing," *Healthcare.gov*.

the difference between the out-of-network fees of a provider and the amount covered by the health insurance of the patient, after deductibles and copays.[218] As per the Department of Health and Human Services, cost sharing occurs when a patient pays for part of healthcare costs that are not covered by health insurance.[219] Cost sharing can be eliminated for COVID-19-related treatment by following lawmakers in DC and Massachusetts.[220] CARES Act appropriations can allow for coverage of reimbursement shortages.

Hence, through triage protocols and staffing shortages, it becomes more probable that patients will use out-of-network providers when they are unable to see the status of their provider's network. Moreover, provider shortages may require that providers fill in care gaps for several conditions, not merely COVID-19, which would allow for the expansion of the potential for surprise medical billing and out-of-network care. Many patients have put off medical care due to fear surrounding the COVID-19 pandemic. For instance, Andrew, an elderly man, experienced persistent leg pain and refused to go to the doctor's office. His therapy dog sensed a problem and howled. When Andrew went to the ED, it turned out that Andrew had heart disease. Andrew is not alone. Nearly half of Americans have reported that either they or a loved one has put off medical care amid the COVID-19 pandemic, according to Consumer Reports.[221]

---

218 Ibid.

219 Andy Bergmann, "CR Survey: The COVID-19 Crisis Has Changed How Americans Live," *Consumer Reports,* December 26, 2020.

220 "Surprise Medical Bills: New Protections for Consumers Take Effect in 2022," *KFF,* February 4, 2021.

221 "Employee Retirement Income Security Act (ERISA)," *US Department of Labor.*

PROTECTION FOR THE FUTURE

Although more than half of US states provide some protection from surprise medical billing, policymakers should eliminate bills from out-of-network providers that exceed the limits of the in-network cost sharing for any and all medical treatments that are received during the COVID-19 pandemic.[222]

In order to ensure comprehensive protections, federal intervention is imperative. The 1974 Employee Retirement Income Security Act (ERISA) prohibits state laws governing health insurance from being applicable to self-insured employer plans—which are generally offered by large employers like Microsoft and Apple.[223] Consequently, current state medical surprise billing protections, coverage mandates, and cost-sharing preventions will not apply to more than half of Americans that have employer-sponsored health insurance—which is nearly 30 percent of the American population.[224] As a result, ERISA leaves millions unprotected by state healthcare reforms.[225] Without a federal response, states may be able to avoid some of the entanglements that arise from ERISA through direct prohibition of providers from charging rates of cost sharing from surprise billing and from COVID-19 treatment.[226]

---

222 Ibid.
223 "Employee Retirement Income Security Act (ERISA)," *US Department of Labor*.
224 Ibid.
225 "Employee Retirement Income Security Act (ERISA)," *US Department of Labor*.
226 Ibid.

However, this approach has been politically unattainable, historically speaking. It may be that the necessary impetus for reform comes from COVID-19.

Never before has the interdependence of all of our health, social fabric, and finances been so visible. Never before has there been a more visible need to improve healthcare, particularly in regard to accessibility. Therefore, our policies in health reform should reflect this, and we should not let the lessons of this pandemic pass us by.

CONCLUSION

- More than 50 percent of Americans with employer-sponsored health insurance received delayed treatment for either themselves or for a loved one in 2019 due to unaffordability.

- The Families First Coronavirus Response Act (FFCRA) mandates all private insurers, Medicaid, Medicare, and Medicare Advantage cover COVID-19 testing costs and, moreover, eliminate cost sharing (coinsurance, copayments, and deductibles) associated with testing services during this time.

- The Coronavirus Aid, Relief, and Economic Security (CARES) Act passed by Congress is a $2.2 trillion pandemic relief bill mandating that all private plans cover the costs of COVID-19 testing and those associated with future vaccinations.

- My policy proposals:

- Policymakers should freeze the insurance status in order to ensure that a maximum number of people are on their existing plan alongside their current providers.

- Policymakers ought to expand access to ACA marketplace plans alongside Medicaid to secure coverage for individuals who have lost their jobs.

- Federal and state officials should continue to address out-of-pocket expenses such as surprise medical billing and cost sharing.

- Policymakers should eliminate bills from out-of-network providers that exceed the limits of the in-network cost sharing for any and all medical treatments that are received during the COVID-19 pandemic.

PART II

STANDARDS OF A TOP-TIER HEALTHCARE SYSTEM

CHAPTER 7

THE CERTAINTY EPIDEMIC

Try this exercise. Read the excerpt below, read the clarifying word, then reread the excerpt. In doing so, pay close attention to your mental state:

A newspaper is better than a magazine. A seashore is a better place than the street. At first it is better to run than to walk. You may have to try several times. It takes some skill but it is easy to learn. Even young children can enjoy it. Once successful, complications are minimal. Birds seldom get too close. Rain, however, soaks in very fast. Too many people doing the same thing can also cause problems. One needs lots of room. If there are no complications it can be very peaceful. A rock will serve as an anchor. If things break loose from it, however, you will not get a second chance.[227]

---

227 "Reading Comprehension Strategies," *Division of Academic Enhacement University of Georgia.*

"Kite."

At a moment's notice, you are inundated with this "aha" moment. Not enough time has elapsed for an evaluation of the change in the mental state. The unconscious mind has sorted through a myriad of possibilities and has been thoroughly convinced that the kite indeed must be the word that fits the excerpt description.

Certainty is omnipotent. Legions of public figures inundate the masses with reasons why certain policies will revolutionize the problems created by other politicians, or the exact moment when life began, or the next uproar of the stock market. The public state of mind has become the national news. Why? Is it because of arrogance or being unreceptive, or is this biologically rooted? Our sense of certainty seems as if it is the only logical conclusion.

However, neurological research has shown this sense of certainty arises from primary neural mechanisms that do not function with pragmatism. Hence, the notion of being certain is not a deliberate choice we make. Rather, it is a sensation that happens to us, as humans.

We all know that emotions are complex. However, there are only six basic emotions—happiness, sadness, anger, disgust, surprise, and fear. Other emotions we have are complex combinations of these emotions. These emotions are associated with the limbic system in the human brain. Certainty is itself an attenuation of surprise.[228]

---

[228] Kendra Cherry, "The 6 Types of Basic Emotions and Their Effect on Human Behavior," *verywellmind*, January 13, 2020.

It is important to recognize this, because knowing this can allow for us to develop a tolerance gradient to consider ideas that are outside the domain of our certainty metrics.

This misguided notion of absolute certainty has led to dreadful and suboptimal results throughout history. Napoleon Bonaparte, the French emperor who conquered much of Europe in the early nineteenth century, had a strong desire to conquer Britain. Bonaparte consequently imposed a trade embargo on Britain.[229] Czar Alexander I of Russia did not comply with Bonaparte, as it would hamper Russian trade.[230] Upon recognizing the dissent the Russians showed, Bonaparte assembled the Grand Armée, one of the largest imperial armies to ever march in war, with nearly five hundred thousand soldiers.[231] Thus far, Bonaparte had been successful since his army was able to survive off the forage due to the rich agriculture in central Europe.[232] Bonaparte, therefore, concluded that his army would once again be successful in Russia.[233] However, Russia had vast barren lands.[234] The Russian army retreated further inland and burned any and all resources to prevent the French army from having access to them.[235] Simply by having a lack of resources for survival, the French army dwindled

---

229 "Napoleon Bonaparte," *History.com,* accessed November 9, 2020.
230 Ibid.
231 "Napoleon Bonaparte," *History.com,* accessed November 9, 2020.
232 Ibid.
233 "Napoleon Bonaparte," *History.com,* accessed November 9, 2020.
234 Ibid.
235 "Napoleon Bonaparte," *History.com,* accessed November 9, 2020.

significantly in size.[236] Faced with dwindled troop counts and lack of amenities, Bonaparte retreated back to France.[237]

In the sports arena, few cricket fans can recollect the Austral-Asia Cup of 1986 between India and Pakistan without a wince.[238] With one wicket in hand, Chetan Sharma, an Indian cricketer, bowled a Yorker.[239] A Yorker is a difficult ball to bowl—so difficult that even many of the best bowlers stray away from bowling it in high-pressure conditions as the one Chetan Sharma was in.[240] As is the case with many bowlers, the ball was a full toss, and Pakistan reigned victorious.[241]

Seen here, Bonaparte's conviction in his militaristic strategy and Chetan Sharma's ambitious yet misguided confidence in a difficult bowl led to their failure. It therefore becomes apparent that an approach to maximizing our absolute certainty of truth is key.

Certainty has the capacity to lead to potentially fatal mistakes, not just embarrassing ones. Skill should be combined with a proven framework and methodology to increase success rates.

A checklist system employs guidelines for both technical and nontechnical requirements for conceivable medical

---

236 Ibid.

237 "Napoleon Bonaparte," *History.com,* accessed November 9, 2020.

238 "Full Scorecard of India vs Pakistan Final 1985/86—Score Report," *ESPN cricinfo.*

239 Ibid.

240 "Full Scorecard of India vs Pakistan Final 1985/86—Score Report," *ESPN cricinfo.*

241 Ibid.

situations. In the case of Isabella from the introduction, a checklist system would have ensured there was no lapse of judgement in patient care. More precisely, the checklist could include keystone items. The goal is to ensure ideal conditions are being observed and both the minuscule and the macroscopic criteria for the ideal conditions are being met in order to maximize the rate at which these ideal conditions are being observed.

In 1935, Boeing set out to give a demonstration of its new airplane. The army asked for certain specifications.[242] Boeing exceeded the requirements for all of these specifications.[243] The plane could travel faster and farther than any plane before it.[244] It had four engines instead of two.[245] Its wingspan was one hundred feet.[246] It was a flying fortress. The plane was supposed to win the bid easily.[247] Boeing was unconcerned as a result and went out ahead toward this necessary step in the bidding process.[248] The major entered the plane.[249] The best pilot in the army at the time then entered the plane.[250] The plane took off three hundred feet above the ground.[251] The

---

242 "Historical Snapshot," *Boeing*.
243 Ibid.
244 "Historical Snapshot," *Boeing*.
245 Ibid.
246 "Historical Snapshot," *Boeing*.
247 Ibid.
248 "Historical Snapshot," *Boeing*.
249 Ibid.
250 "Historical Snapshot," *Boeing*.
251 Ibid.

plane came down and crashed, killing the pilot and almost bankrupting Boeing.[252]

What was going on? Was this plane unflyable? Boeing soon realized that the answer was not more training; the person who flew the plane was the most well-trained in the army at the time.[253] The Boeing Model 299 crash was not because of some structural failure or malfunctioning of any of the four engines.[254] Rather, the crash was due to the locked conditions of the rudder and elevator surface controls.[255] These two factors, mainly the latter, resulted in the pilot being unable to control the airplane.[256] After some evaluation, Boeing soon realized they needed a simple checklist to make sure all rather obvious tasks were being checked for.[257] The locked conditions of the rudder and elevator surface controls were due to the possibility that the pilot had only partially depressed prior to takeoff, and given the system was malfunctioning, the pilot did not fully disengage the locking pin.[258] Alternatively, there was no effort made to unlock the controls prior to takeoff, and as a result the controls were fully locked.[259]

---

252 "Historical Snapshot," *Boeing*.
253 Ibid.
254 "Historical Snapshot," *Boeing*.
255 Ibid.
256 "Historical Snapshot," *Boeing*.
257 Ibid.
258 "Historical Snapshot," *Boeing*.
259 Ibid.

Van Halen was the first band to go into smaller markets.[260] Typically, Van Halen would come in with three eighteen-wheelers and a much larger production value.[261] The smaller markets had less sophistication.[262] The contract had more than a hundred items that needed to be crossed off before Van Halen could show up for the show.[263] In this very thick contract, there was Article 126—the "no brown M&Ms" clause.[264] So if Van Halen arrives and gets ready to go on stage for their rehearsal, the contract team would look at the bowl of M&Ms, and if the bowl of M&Ms had a brown M&M, Van Halen would cancel their show.[265]

More specifically, Van Halen would do a walk-through to ensure everything was done right.[266] This is because if the group that was putting on the event could not get the brown M&Ms clause correct, they also probably made mistakes elsewhere.[267] For instance, the stage for the con-

---

260 Julie Zeveloff, "There's a brilliant reason why Van Halen asked for a bowl of M&Ms with all the brown candies removed before every show," *Insider*, September 6, 2016.

261 Ibid.

262 Ibid.

263 Julie Zeveloff, "There's a brilliant reason why Van Halen asked for a bowl of M&Ms with all the brown candies removed before every show," *Insider*, September 6, 2016.

264 Ibid.

265 Julie Zeveloff, "There's a brilliant reason why Van Halen asked for a bowl of M&Ms with all the brown candies removed before every show," *Insider*, September 6, 2016.

266 Ibid.

267 Julie Zeveloff, "There's a brilliant reason why Van Halen asked for a bowl of M&Ms with all the brown candies removed before every show," *Insider*, September 6, 2016.

cert could have been placed incorrectly, resulting in severe injuries to a band such as Van Halen.[268] Hence, precautions were implemented.[269] Despite being mundane and seemingly irrelevant, the "no brown M&Ms" clause was absolutely essential.[270]

However, this "no brown M&Ms" clause can be applied to all of our lives. It is about mastering the basics to ensure that not only are other basics mastered, but also that there is sufficient confidence for the advanced items being done correctly.

A keystone is the stone that blocks the arch. Hence, the keystone allows for the arch to maintain its stability. Researchers on habit building, the science of building effective habits, focus often on keystone habits. Keystone habits are the activities you do that most benefit you.[271] The goal is to identify these keystone habits and put them on a checklist to have a checklist embodying the "no brown M&Ms" clause.

The ideal way to put keystone habits onto a checklist is to consider it under the context of a masterpiece day. Good checklists are often created at pause points. In the aviation industry, there are pause points such as before takeoff, during

---

268 Ibid.

269 Julie Zeveloff, "There's a brilliant reason why Van Halen asked for a bowl of M&Ms with all the brown candies removed before every show," *Insider*, September 6, 2016.

270 Ibid.

271 Julie Zeveloff, "There's a brilliant reason why Van Halen asked for a bowl of M&Ms with all the brown candies removed before every show," *Insider*, September 6, 2016.

taxi, and before landing.[272] We all have three pause points in our masterpiece days as well—the a.m. time block, the p.m. time block, and the cycles within our days. Thus, keystone checklists can be created for each of these pause points.

It is important to clarify that these keystone checklists, despite their thoroughness, should not be multiple pages long. Rather, these checklists should be on the magnitude of an index card—a few words for a box.

In healthcare, it is important that mental preoccupation with certainty be replaced with checklists. A checklist is an embodiment of a systemic approach for reducing errors and thereby increasing the chances of achieving the ideal outcome.[273] In order to create a "good" checklist, here are five suggestions:

1. Keep it concise.

2. Break down tasks into subtasks that are achievable on their own.

3. Make it either:

    a. READ-and-DO (read the list and do the task), or

    b. CHECK-and-DO (confirmation of tasks listed).

---

272 "Flight Safety, discipline, and importance of checklists," *BAA Training*. September 25, 2017.

273 Ibid.

4. Keep updating it.

5. Have "pause points" (points at which one runs through the list before proceeding).

CONCLUSION
- A checklist system employs guidelines for both technical and nontechnical requirements for conceivable medical situations.

- The "no brown M&Ms" clause is about mastering the basics to ensure that not only are other basics mastered, but also that there is sufficient confidence for the advanced items being done correctly.

- The goal is to identify keystone habits and put them on a checklist to have a checklist embodying the "no brown M&Ms" clause.

CHAPTER 8

ACHIEVING OPENNESS AND NATIONAL DISCUSSION

There are pressing issues that require urgent action, and they are a direct result of not anticipating these issues. When these problems are acted upon, resources are extracted from areas that are far more important in the long run. Issues such as organizational development are impacted. In a society where there is rapid change, increased foresight is essential for collective success.

There are four choices we all face when discussing the future:

1. **Be Reactive:** This is where one would wait to hear the fire alarm to extinguish the fire visibly there.

2. **Be Passive:** The passive actor is someone who recognizes there is a need for change but does not challenge it.

3. **Be Prepared:** They believe in the notion that an ounce of prevention is worth a pound of cure.

4. **Provoke the Change Desired:** This is where one is proactive in seeking change.

In healthcare, there are two scenarios. The one we are currently in favors a reactive strategy. This is because we are in a crisis. How do we know we are in a crisis? Well, one way to quantitatively measure how healthy a country is can be seen through the life expectancy at birth. In the year 1959, the life expectancy in the United States was 69.9 years. It rose to 79.1 years in 2014. However, the life expectancy has been dropping since 2015.[274]

In the 1950s, the United States was ranked in the top ten countries for life expectancy, but now we do not even rank in the top thirty.[275] There has been a clear shift from a collective focus to one where we have to get treatment as individuals. As a society, we have increased income inequality, and this results in increased stress, contributing to a far worse health outcome.

The United States currently does not invest nearly enough in early-life care. Disease risk such as for lung and heart disease is programmed in the early life, particularly the first thousand days post-conception.[276] You cannot simply put a stent in a coronary artery to redress stress that came from a

---

274 Max Roser, Esteban Ortiz-Ospina, and Hannah Ritchie, "Life Expectancy," *Our World in Data*. 2013.

275 Ibid.

276 Cyrus Cooper, Elizabeth Cottrell, Elsie M. Taveras, and Maynika V. Rastogi, "The First 1,000 Days: Early Life Determinants of Chronic Disease," *Endocrine News*, July 2014.

lack of support from parents in early life. This is why it is very important to have paid maternity leave as a national policy. Furthermore, the United States has the most child poverty when compared to all other developed countries.

Inequality kills! There are several accompanying negative outcomes that can manifest themselves in the form of stress, abuse, and rage. Stress can promote alcohol and drug use, and this contributes to the rising mortality rate.

Even when comparing the life expectancy of wealthy individuals, according to the UNDP Human Development Reports, the life expectancy is higher in Europe.[277] This is a manifestation of the social pain.

Spending more money is not the solution. Clearly, the United States is spending more money on healthcare than any other country in the world.[278] Rather, it is far more advantageous to increase the social spending. Specifically, a possible solution is that the money could come by decreasing income inequality by taxing the wealthy more.

According to a study done at Yale University by Professor Elizabeth Bradley, countries in better health emphasize social spending.[279] In contrast, the United States prioritizes medical care spending. Hence, by subsidizing education,

---

277 "Life expectancy at birth (years)," *United Nations Development Programme Human Development Reports*, 2013.

278 Ibid.

279 E.H. Bradley, H. Sipsma, and L.A. Taylor, "American health care paradox - high spending on health care and poor health," *QJM: An International Journal of Medicine* 110, no. 2, October 24, 2016.

transportation, and housing, inequality can be reduced, providing a means of improving US healthcare.

Another study, done by Harvard Professor Jason Beckfield, highlighted that if the United States had the average level of social spending of countries that are in the OECD such as Germany, Canada, and Australia, there would be an increase of more than 3.7 years in life expectancy.[280]

Lastly, several models by the Institute for Health Metrics and Evaluation predict that the US ranking for life expectancy will fall to sixty-fourth by the year 2040.[281] Hence, it is of utmost importance that we, as a society, take note to consider implementing alternative strategies for improving healthcare.

OPPORTUNITIES FOR TAKING CHARGE OF YOUR OWN CARE: One of the major cited concerns of patients is not having enough involvement in their *own* care. The lack of openness with patients about their treatment is what demonstrates the US healthcare system is focused on reactive healthcare instead of preventive healthcare.

The most significant driver in rising healthcare costs is chronic illnesses, many of which are preventable.[282] Hence, the current

---

280 Jason Beckfield and Clare Bambra, "Shorter lives in stingier states: Social policy shortcomings help explain the US mortality disadvantage," *ScienceDirect* 171, October 18, 2016.

281 Susan Perry, "U.S. life expectancy ranking will plummet by 2040, researchers predict," *MinnPost*, October 19, 2018.

282 "Health and Economic Costs of Chronic Diseases," *Centers for Disease Control and Prevention,* January 12, 2021.

trend of shorter therapeutic encounters between patients and their doctors is not, in fact, dominating US healthcare costs.

The question then becomes: How can national discussion and openness influence a patient's ability to prevent their medical concerns and be a more effective contributor to the healthcare system?

Arguably, the greatest opportunity comes from the internet. There is abundant information on healthy habits and disease prevention. Some of the information is factually accurate and some is not. It is quite apparent there is a double-edged sword of openness. Most people do not have the tools for effectively evaluating the information. Yet, equally important is the fact that there is very little transparency in regard to the source of where the information is coming from. There is a very dire need for comprehensive, factually-backed, consumer-friendly, and relevant medical information. In addition, there should be quality measures to allow for better judgement of the information.

When viewed through a lens of openness, patients are arguably the most important source of information *for* the healthcare system. Patients serve as the most direct piece of evidence on their condition, and with their recollections, the most immediate source of information can be provided.

There are several ways patients can help improve healthcare and allow for a shift toward preventive healthcare. One way is to participate in research studies. Patients are involved in gathering information for the most cutting-edge research and finding solicitations of many clinical trials. One such case is Olivia's decision to participate in a clinical trial when she was diagnosed with breast cancer.

Olivia visited her doctor for a mammogram, and there was nothing of concern. A few months later, Olivia went in for a routine checkup with another doctor. While the physical exam was normal, a large breast tumor was found, indicative of breast cancer. With further consults from other doctors, Olivia ended up at a cancer center. There, Dr. Anderson noted:

> *Two rounds of chemotherapy, surgery, radiation, perhaps some additional chemotherapy, followed by hormonal therapy.*

Dr. Anderson also happened to be a principal investigator at the cancer center, where he was conducting a study on why it is that some breast cancers respond to paclitaxel chemotherapy while others do not.

Paclitaxel chemotherapy is used to treat early-stage breast cancer, often in combination with other chemotherapy drugs.

Since Olivia was scheduled to receive paclitaxel chemotherapy and also fit the criteria of the study, Dr. Anderson asked if Olivia would be willing to be a part of this clinical trial study.

There are different types of clinical trials. Some test new drugs and focus on novel approaches to treatment, whereas others refine existing treatments. Dr. Anderson was focused on the latter. In the case of Olivia, the study involved switching the order of the two chemotherapy drugs that Olivia was to receive as part of the standard treatment in an effort to see the impact this may have on the tumors.

Clearly, this was of interest to Dr. Anderson for his study. It was less clear how much immediate value Olivia would gain from this study. Regardless, Olivia readily agreed to join this clinical trial study.

Olivia was intrigued by the different chemotherapy drugs and the impact on the tumors.

For a quarter of a year, Olivia received paclitaxel chemotherapy, and, in fact, her tumor did shrink.

The information gained from clinical trial studies is immeasurable—not necessarily for the patient but rather for the patient community who may be suffering from a similar condition some time down the line.

Patient activism can help speed up research development. However, at this point in time, the potential of patient input is just starting to get noticed. Evidentially, patient recorded outcomes (PROs) are being seen as increasingly important for clinical trials.[283] PROs provide the patient's perspective on how a particular medical intervention impacted them. Additionally, through an increase in patient participation in choosing medical treatments and interventions, patients are able to receive preference-sensitive

---

283 Rebecca Mercieca-Bebber, Madeleine T. King, Melanie J. Calvert, Martin R. Stockler, and Michael Friedlander, "The importance of patient-reported outcomes in clinical trials and strategies for future optimization," *Dovepress Patient Related Outcome Measures* 9, November 1, 2018.

care. In doing so, there has been a 23 percent reduction in both expensive and invasive treatments.[284]

Through remote monitoring, digital technologies can enable more data to be collected to allow for increased treatment when data collection is being performed. Likewise, telemedicine is becoming increasingly common to allow for patients to be connected to medical centers to conduct diagnostically relevant information or even conduct consults.[285]

Having greater access to medical information and thereby having informed healthcare consumers means that healthcare prices can drop and quality can be improved. It is essentially impossible for a market to function when there is no information about either the cost or the quality. In the healthcare industry, information about cost and quality is largely not available to the general public.

The Department of Homeland Security asks US citizens when they see something, to say something in regard to suspicious behavior. This is a way for all Americans to do their part in protecting their country. However, according to a study published in the Health Affairs Journal by Toffolutti and Stuckler, "A Culture of Openness Is Associated with Lower Mortality Rates among 137 English National Health Service Acute Trusts," this level of vigilance and openness is useful in the healthcare setting as well.[286] Hospital openness

---

284 Ibid.

285 "Medicare Telemedicine Health Care Provider Fact Sheet," Centers for Medicare & Medicaid Services, March 17, 2020.

286 Veronica Toffolutti and David Stuckler, "A Culture of Openness Is Associated With Lower Mortality Rates Among 137 English National Health Service Acute Trusts," *Health Affairs* 38, no. 5, May 2019.

is essentially an environment where the "see something, say something" ideology is implemented.[287] The study found that by having this level of vigilance and openness in the healthcare setting, both patient safety and the goals for the care of patients were improved.[288] Moreover, the study examined data from hospitals in the United Kingdom between 2012 and 2014 and looked at the mortality rates across hospitals that utilized vigilant openness in the healthcare setting.[289] The study supported the conclusion that vigilant openness does indeed reduce mortality rates.[290] However, the study was able to attribute this indication of reduced mortality rates to the implementation of a system where incidents can be reported.[291] Hence, shifting a defensive healthcare environment to one where providers are taking responsibility for their mistakes can accelerate the shift toward vigilant openness.

These aforementioned assumptions are the basis for establishing consumer-directed health plans (CDHP). In brief, these plans allow for healthcare patients and consumers to be able to make informed decisions about buying. Through these plans, members have the ability to use medical payment accounts such as health savings accounts (HSAs) or health

---

287 Ibid.

288 Veronica Toffolutti and David Stuckler, "A Culture of Openness Is Associated With Lower Mortality Rates Among 137 English National Health Service Acute Trusts," *Health Affairs* 38, no. 5, May 2019.

289 Ibid.

290 Veronica Toffolutti and David Stuckler, "A Culture of Openness Is Associated With Lower Mortality Rates Among 137 English National Health Service Acute Trusts," *Health Affairs* 38, no. 5, May 2019.

291 Ibid.

reimbursement accounts. The members are also protected from high-cost medical expenses.

According to a 2006 study done by Goodman, CDHP patients are two times as likely to ask about costs as patients who are in otherwise traditional plans.[292] In addition, CDHP patients are three times as likely to choose a treatment option that is less costly.[293] Lastly, the study found that patients with chronic conditions are 20 percent more likely to follow the treatment process more carefully.[294] Over the long term, it is consequently expected that using HSAs and other medical payment accounts will allow for Americans to pay less since these payment accounts will increase the number of free-market variables that are present in the healthcare system. As a result, there will be increased competition, and this can allow for lower prices and high quality of care simultaneously. However, in the current practice of healthcare insurance, it is overly optimistic to think that most of the people who are insured will become skilled at shopping in the healthcare industry.

It is important to recognize that while greater openness is imperative, decision support systems (DSS) are designed to replace the insights that diagnosticians may provide. Decision support tools are needed now more than ever before. DSSs are information systems that support the organization

---

292 John Goodman, "Consumer Directed Health Care," *Networks Financial Institute at Indiana State University*. December 2006.

293 Ibid.

294 John Goodman, "Consumer Directed Health Care," *Networks Financial Institute at Indiana State University*. December 2006.

processes.²⁹⁵ These systems gather, analyze, and synthesize the patient data to produce reports that are comprehensive.²⁹⁶ According to a study by Walter F. Steward in 2007, "Bridging the Inferential Gap: The Electronic Health Record and Clinical Evidence," there are over ten thousand conditions known, and there are more than two thousand clinical guidelines for practicing.²⁹⁷ Currently, these decision support tools have very limited capabilities because they are not very inclusive. Many, if not most, of these decision support tools are not able to take a comprehensive approach covering drugs to the preferences that patients may have.

Moreover, many physicians cease to listen to patients prematurely, and this has likely implications on the quality of diagnosis. According to a study by Landro, "Preventing the Tragedy of Misdiagnosis," misdiagnoses account for about 60 percent of malpractice claims and misdiagnosis levels nationally are at 30 percent.²⁹⁸ Hence, it becomes apparent that decision support systems are becoming increasingly needed.

Through clinical consultations, patients often detail they are not fully aware of all medical procedure options and their accompanied consequences. Through the use of decision

---

295 Troy Segal, "Decision Support System - DSS," *Investopedia*. June 27, 2020.

296 Ibid.

297 Walter F. Steward, Nirav R. Shah, Mark J. Selna, Ronald A. Paulus, and James M. Walker, "Bridging the Inferential Gap: The Electronic Health Record and Clinical Evidence Emerging tools can help physicians bridge the gap between knowledge they possess and knowledge they do not," *Health Affairs*. 26, no. 2, January 26, 2007.

298 Laura Landro, "Preventing the tragedy of misdiagnosis," *Pittsburgh Post-Gazette*, November 28, 2006.

support interventions, the gap in communication between providers and patients can be improved. The problem, however, is that decision support interventions are available to very few medical decisions daily.

In addition, there are several other factors that contribute to the lack of openness in healthcare. One of these barriers is the perception of a difficult patient. The label of being difficult is given if there is a conflict between what the patient believes and the clinical decision process itself. However, through a system that empowers patients to question healthcare providers on their own care, openness can be more readily achieved. Questions such as a simple curiosity about the medical procedure can start a dialogue that paves the way for further conversation in regard to patient care between the provider and the patient. Next, the patient may ask about the consequences of several options detailed by the provider. Lastly and most importantly, the patient asks the provider on how the patient can contribute to improving medical intervention outcomes.

Moving toward the future, the implementation of openness in healthcare is of ever-growing importance and a necessity for proper care, especially with the increased use of artificial intelligence (AI). Openness in healthcare with increased AI use can mean several things. For one, this can refer to the source code for programming languages, the accessibility to data, safety measures, and organizational goals. Thus, by developing an AI healthcare strategy and defining goals, initiatives, and resource allocation, it can be ensured that proper scaling of AI solutions are effectively implemented.

A particularly useful AI tool would be in care delivery. Advances such as voice technology and digital assistants would pave the way for increased accuracy and precision in healthcare. Some of the benefits include having more time for preparation for consultations, rapid and accurate diagnosis, and, most importantly, increased transparency in patient care.

Bionic Pancreas is an AI care delivery tool that utilizes machine learning to monitor and manage the blood sugar levels in patients with type 1 diabetes.[299] At the present moment, providers have to teach the patients who use an insulin pump or who manually inject insulin how to count carbohydrate intake.[300] The problem with this is having a very large range where mistakes can be made in the process.[301] With the use of a Bionic Pancreas, this would not be required.[302] Moreover, there would be a lot more time available for the providers and patients to focus on having a more transparent discussion of the healthcare for the patient.[303]

Hospitals at large also benefit from care delivery, as this would enable a shift toward value-based healthcare, a system in which providers and the hospitals are paid based on the patient health outcomes rather than on the amount of healthcare service being delivered to the patient. In brief,

---

299 "Artificial pancreas helps children with type 1 diabetes," *National Institutes of Health*, September 15, 2020.

300 Ibid.

301 "Artificial pancreas helps children with type 1 diabetes," *National Institutes of Health*, September 15, 2020.

302 Ibid.

303 "Artificial pancreas helps children with type 1 diabetes," *National Institutes of Health*, September 15, 2020.

there are several benefits to this approach. The patient gets to enjoy lower costs and better health outcomes. The providers enjoy the higher patient satisfaction rates and have better efficiencies in providing care. The payers have reduced risks and stronger cost controls. The suppliers enjoy an alignment of the prices associated with the patient outcome. Lastly, society as a whole benefits through better overall health and reduced healthcare spending.

Another example exists with virtual assistants, especially for effective chronic disease modulation and personalized monitoring for follow-up healthcare. Through virtual assistants, there is increased customizability and personalization. Payers can benefit through the increased patient adherence to care as the patient is far more engaged through this personalized medicine tool. Furthermore, the payers may even allow for early interventions to prevent risks, thereby marking a shift toward preventive medicine to allow for the reduction of avoidable hospitalizations. Lastly, policymakers can also reap benefits: wellness information can be provided, as well as increased support for monitoring of clinical trials or patient education and increased pharmaceutical adherence.

Through the use of risk prediction for hospital admissions, patients who are at risk of unplanned hospital admission can be identified from a given population. Risk prediction would work through machine learning algorithms to allow for data mining for predictive measures to be implemented. This can allow for the enabling of various protocols in varying risk levels. As a result, there is a shift from reactive to preventive care through this process as well.

However, for proper use of risk prediction models, it is important for providers and social workers to understand how exactly the model identifies the patient and, more importantly, the factors that need to be addressed in an effort to mitigate the risk in the future. Through this process, unnecessary hospital admissions can be reduced.

Reactive healthcare is where a patient reacts to a condition by visiting a doctor. Depending on what the diagnosis of the condition is, the doctor prescribes a medication. In this case, both the patient and the doctor are reacting to the condition.

As of now, healthcare costs more than $3 trillion every year.[304] This is more than two times as much as the cost of healthcare in other developed countries.[305] Reactive healthcare encourages visits to the doctor when conditions have become visibly severe. Many of these conditions could have been detected far earlier by emphasizing healthy habits.

This is why preventive healthcare is so important in reducing healthcare costs. In preventive healthcare, rather than waiting to see your doctor until the condition becomes severe, you are proactively involved in maintaining your health.

There are three levels of preventive healthcare. Primary prevention involves providing healthcare before a condition onset. Here are some ways you can not only stay healthier but also contribute to a much more cost-effective healthcare system:

---

304 "Health and Economic Costs of Chronic Diseases," *Centers for Disease Control and Prevention,* January 12, 2021.

305 Ibid.

- Get regular checkups with your doctor. This will allow you to have a consistent measure of your health, thereby minimizing the chances that some expected condition becomes severe enough to cause considerable harm.

- Keep physically active—exercise regularly and sufficiently.

- Wash the food you purchase at the supermarket.

- Refrain from drugs and alcohol.

- Sleep regularly.

Secondary prevention is done when some concerning signs are observed. In this case, doctors may order some preliminary screenings and scans.

Lastly, tertiary prevention is essentially proactive treatment given that the condition is severe enough to warrant immediate procedural action. The outcomes from tertiary prevention are far more grim than secondary or primary prevention.

CONCLUSION

- How can national discussion and openness influence a patient's ability to prevent their medical concerns and be a more effective contributor to the healthcare system?

- Shifting a defensive healthcare environment to one where providers are taking responsibility for their mistakes can accelerate the shift toward vigilant openness.

- Moving toward the future, the implementation of openness in healthcare is of ever-growing importance and a necessity for proper care, especially with the increased use of artificial intelligence (AI).

CHAPTER 9

PRINCIPLES OF A VALUE-BASED SYSTEM

In *The Godfather Part II*, Vito Corleone collapses in the rose garden, and shortly after, Anthony, his grandson, runs to find help. A watering gun is depicted in this scene to represent power. Vito is struggling with the idea of having to give his power, status, and business to Michael, his son. Michael had no choice but to become the new owner of his father's business.

This scene is an iconic representation of what hospitals are experiencing right now. Vito Corleone is analogous to the insurance business, and hospitals are like Michael, who has no option. The boundaries that exist between being a provider and being a payer are becoming blurred as hospitals incur increasing risk. In essence, being the CEO of a hospital is like being the CEO of an insurance company.

Fundamentally, in order to obtain results, both the quality of service and reliability are of utmost importance; and at baseline, this can be achieved when all parties are on the same page. Healthcare is complicated, with stakeholders having not only varied goals but often conflicting ones as well. These issues include profitability, containment of cost, the quality of care, and convenience, among other factors. Currently, there is a lot of opacity about everyone's goals, and due to this, the healthcare system is gamed, taking unfair advantage of people: Everyone pulls strings in their direction, and over time this string becomes worn out and breaks.

There has been an increasing emphasis on providing quality care for patients. However, the problem is that the value provided is questionable to say the least. Quality, here, is defined as health outcomes based on dollars as the proxy variable. Value ought to define healthcare performance and its improvement over time. The most effective way to drive progress in the healthcare system is to have a rigorous measure of value. Currently, however, value is so loosely defined that it is misunderstood and remains unmeasured for the most part.

In a healthcare system that is well functioning, the concept of value should be centered around the patient, and it should be the value patients receive that determines the rewards for all other actors in the healthcare system. Hence, value should not depend on the volume of services being delivered. The shift from volume to value is a challenge. The process of care used is not a means of measuring value, particularly in relation to the measurement of results and associated costs.

Value can be thought of as efficiency. When prices decline yet there is no consideration for the outcomes, this is self-defeating, leading to limitations in the care provided.

When considered mathematically, the numerator of the value equation is outcomes and the denominator is costs. For any medical condition, outcome is multidimensional. There is no given outcome that can precisely provide the results of care. Costs in healthcare are not merely the costs of individualistic services; rather, costs refer to the aggregate costs of the entire duration for a patient's medical care. In order for costs to be lowered, it is often best to spend more on certain services such that other services are less needed.

None of the organizational units that comprise healthcare delivery reflect the boundaries in which value is created. A proper unit of measuring value needs to account for all of the services that determine success in terms of a patient's medical care. If a patient has diabetes, value would mean that care would integrate the care for conditions such as hypertension and vascular disease.

In the context of preventative care, value needs to be measured based on similarity. This can be accorded into categories such as healthy adults, patients with only one chronic condition, and elderly patients.

Typically, medical care involves several specialties, and therefore there is significant intervention. As a result, in order for any particular intervention to be beneficial to the patient, it is important for other interventions to be effective in the context of the entire care cycle for a patient. Accountability for value, therefore, needs to be shared among all those involved in the care of a patient. Instead of the current *focus factories*, which focus on a narrow range of medical interventions, there needs to be a shift toward the integration of practices that allow for aggregate accountability for the overall care of a patient's medical condition.

Since medical care activities are interdependent, revelations on *value* appear only with due time and are manifested through outcomes such as recovery or worsening health. By longitudinally tracking the outcomes of a patient's health and associated costs, accurate measurements of value can be made.

Patients who have multiple medical conditions should have each and every condition measured for value separately while accounting for the presence of said other medical conditions to account for risk adjustment. Doing so will allow for comparisons to be made.

The current method of healthcare delivery makes it difficult to deliver value and measure it. As a result, the vast majority of providers fail to deliver value. Providers generally measure only what they directly control in their office instead of outcomes. For instance, current measures look at a particular department or the entire hospital. In both cases, the goldilocks zone, or the ideal middle zone, is missed and fails to be useful for patients. Moreover, costs are measured for billing units rather than the full cycle of care for the patient. This helps to explain why providers do not accept responsibility for outcomes, often blaming their lack of control on outside factors and/or on the compliance of patients.

Quality means adhering to a set of guidelines that have been rigorously analyzed, and the measurement of quality focuses on the processes that concern care. The Healthcare

Effectiveness Data and Information Set (HEDIS) measures the most widely used quality measurement system.[306] Within the HEDIS, all except five measures are process measures, and none of them are actual outcomes.[307] It is important to recognize that although process measurement is useful for various healthcare institutions, it is in no way a substitute for measuring outcomes. Within any complex system, an attempt to engage in behavioral control with no results measured hinders progress to increments. There is no substitute for measuring true outcomes, whose main purpose are to allow for innovations in healthcare, not merely a comparison of providers. This negative feedback loop enables providers to have the information to consistently improve in order to allow for innovations to flourish.

ELEMENTS OF VALUE

The central driver of valuable improvement is measuring outcomes. This is apparent in organ transplantations, where there is universal outcome measurement. In order to get an organ transplanted, the outcome needs to be reported. Secondly, this is observed in *in vitro* fertilizations. Per federal law, every clinic is mandated to report every case to the Centers for Disease Control and Prevention (CDC).[308] Analyzing these two areas—reporting the outcomes through increased transparency—the improvement process has

---

306 "HEDIS and Performance Management," *NCQA*.

307 Ibid.

308 "Mandatory Reporting of Infectious Diseases by Clinicians," *CDC*, June 22, 1990.

skyrocketed.[309] This is the law of nature. These analyses are universal.

Having worked in depth in healthcare delivery in the United States, the United Kingdom, Sweden, Denmark, and various other countries, Michael Porter, the Bishop William Lawrence University professor at Harvard Business School, finds that although insurance is highly different across the world, the problems of delivery are virtually identical.[310] In an interview with Stefan Larsson, Porter shares his insight on how a shift toward value-based healthcare can be made.[311]

Currently, we have a zero-sum competition in healthcare. People in healthcare are attempting to get more money from one source, getting higher reimbursements and pushing past costs to the patients. This is *not* the way forward. By creating a positive-sum competition, providing value will allow for all parties involved to win.

Michael illuminates the scenario of a patient being blindfolded and being taken to a hospital in a different country from the United States: it would look the same.[312] This is because the organization of these issues are a function of the same fundamental level of training, the same way that medical science has developed over time, the same

---

309   Ibid.

310   "What Matters Most: Patient Outcomes and the Transformation of Health Care," *ICHOM*.

311   Ibid.

312   "What Matters Most: Patient Outcomes and the Transformation of Health Care," *ICHOM*.

way that providers are trained in medical school and residency programs.

Michael describes the three most pertinent barriers preventing this shift to value-based healthcare.[313] First, the mindset and ability to look at different perspectives is a hinderance.[314] For instance, many individuals in the healthcare industry believe the problem at large is about reducing costs and not about improving value.[315] Second, there is a critical lack of both outcome data and understanding costs.[316] Finally, there is a lot of misalignment of the stakeholders because the incentive structure tends to pit parties against one another.[317] Michael warns that if the US healthcare system is not reformed to a value-based system, costs will continue to skyrocket.[318] Random reimbursement cuts will be made and care will be rationed, among other chaotic issues.[319] Michael, therefore, warns there is an urgent need for more evidence-based data on the outcome and cost sides.[320] Particularly, there should be an emphasis accelerating on the impact of outcome

---

313 Ibid.

314 "What Matters Most: Patient Outcomes and the Transformation of Health Care," *ICHOM*.

315 Ibid.

316 "What Matters Most: Patient Outcomes and the Transformation of Health Care," *ICHOM*.

317 Ibid.

318 "What Matters Most: Patient Outcomes and the Transformation of Health Care," *ICHOM*.

319 Ibid.

320 "What Matters Most: Patient Outcomes and the Transformation of Health Care," *ICHOM*.

measurement on progress.[321] The ability to pull together what is known about outcomes in ten or fifteen of the most important medical conditions will be an enormous accelerator for progress.

AN INTERVIEW WITH DR. STEPHEN SONNENBERG

Dr. Stephen Sonnenberg, professor at UT Austin Dell Medical School, put it this way in an interview I held with him: We, as a society, need to think collectively about healthcare. People who have healthcare take it for granted. People who do not have it put their hands up in the air and say they never can have it. Many problems, as later pointed out, are hidden despite being right in front of us.

The largest purveyors of mental healthcare in the United States are jails and prisons. Jails and prisons are not equipped for this. Drugs are often bought through a secret black market. Some causes are social and psychiatric, not simply biological. Dr. Sonnenberg assets that political diatribes, such as the adoption of a system that encourages narrowmindedness in the George W. Bush era, prevent us as a society from recognizing that there is a mental healthcare crisis currently imminent. This encourages people to become fearful, and in the process, a lot of resources are wasted toward an advocation that merits no actual resolution. This is not merely a penal system issue; rather, this is a systemic healthcare problem. We are not living in a democratic society that encourages people to be generous; rather, people are rewarded for being selfish.

---

321 Ibid.

When President Obama was attempting to enact the Affordable Care Act (ACA), there was interesting opposition—opposition from the Republican Party from politicians who were, on average, more economically advantaged than the Democratic Party base. This resulted in fearmongering over the idea that healthcare must be rationed, and the ACA would be analogous to a death squad determining what people can get what care. This eloquently speaks to the core fundamentals of democracy. We, as a society, have lost sight of the core democratic principle, which is to provide the most for the most.

If we are to recognize healthcare as a thematic concept that is democratic at its very core, we will need to begin to reprioritize how money is spent and also how taxing is done the United States. Only about 20 percent of health is what happens in the doctor's office. Eighty percent of health is structural. Looked at from an ethical perspective, and not simply medical ethics—rather the broad score from considerations of the US Constitution, the Bill of Rights, and the United Nations—healthcare is a human right.

Making rationed choices about lowering costs is dependent on the measurement, reporting, and comparison of outcomes. In order to determine which outcomes to measure for a given medical condition, there are several principles that need to be followed. The outcomes should account for the health circumstances relevant to the patient, account for short-term and long-term care, and consider risk factors. Due to the complexity of medicine and healthcare, success is dependent on outcomes being weighed against one another. For instance, this may involve a comparison of short-term safety with long-term functionality.

For any given medical condition, outcomes can be arrayed in a hierarchy. Tier one is the health status that is achieved, with the exception of patients with degenerative conditions, in which case it is the health status retained. The first level is survival, and for most patients survival is the most important outcome. The second level looks at the gradient of recovery. Here, considerations look at the functional status and degree of autonomy. Tier two is focused on the recovery phase. The first level in tier two looks at the time required to achieve a state of normalcy. The second level looks at the short-term complications involved in the treatment process. Tier three is health sustainability. The first level in tier three looks at long-term complications. The second level looks at health processes that arise from the treatment phase of the care.

Efforts looking at measurement need to begin with at least one outcome in each of the tiers, and preferably at each level within each of the tiers.

From this interview, I believe that the inability to prioritize value improvement in providing healthcare and measuring the quality of care through *value* has resulted in poor cost containment, hindered innovation, and micromanaging of medical practices. By enabling a means of measuring value, the reimbursement system can be reformed such that value is rewarded through bundled payments covering the entire cycle of care. Through this, providers can be rewarded for efficiency in achieving positive outcomes and, in the process, create a standard of accountability.

FUTURE STEPS

As a medical scribe, I have noticed that, from the perspective of the patient, outcomes can be dire.

Harry was sixty-six years old when he experienced a stroke causing him to have difficulties in bodily movements on his right side. Harry was able to get dressed but abnormally slowly. When Harry went to the geriatric rehabilitation ward, he went with high hopes that he would regain his normal level of independence. However, that is not what happened: his condition deteriorated such that he did not regain his normal level of independence.

Outcome measures defined by healthcare providers do not consistently align with those desired by patients or even relevant to what they want. The addition of patient-reported outcome measures would be a promising measure, as it would increase data availability on what patients are expecting from their care and treatment.

With the usage of value-based healthcare services, relevant outcomes ought to move toward a higher state of quality. However, before moving toward such a state, several factors need to be considered. First, when developing patient-reported outcome and experiential measures, a means of standardizing needs to be established such that evaluation at an aggregate level can be done. Secondly, strategies need to be considered that will allow for the relating of outcomes to performances. Currently, in the fragmented healthcare system that exists, this is of particular need. This can be accomplished by increasing collaboration beyond organizational boundaries such that clear trajectories for patients can be established.

CONCLUSION

- The most effective way to drive progress in the healthcare system is to have a rigorous measure of value.

- Instead of the current *focus factories*, which focus on a narrow range of medical interventions, there needs to be a shift toward the integration of practices that allow for aggregate accountability for the overall care of a patient's medical condition.

- The most pertinent barriers preventing this shift to value-based healthcare are:

  - The mindset and ability to look at different perspectives is a hindrance;

  - There is a critical lack of both outcome data and understanding costs; and

  - There is a lot of misalignment of the stakeholders because the incentive structure tends to pit parties against one another.

- The inability to prioritize value improvement in providing healthcare and measuring the quality of care through *value* has resulted in poor cost containment, hindered innovation, and micromanaging of medical practices.

- By enabling a means of measuring value, the reimbursement system can be reformed such that value is rewarded through bundled payments covering the entire cycle of care.

- Considerations before shifting to a value-based system:

    - When developing patient-reported outcome and experiential measures, a means of standardizing needs to be established such that evaluation at an aggregate level can be done; and

    - Strategies need to be considered that will allow for the relating of outcomes to performances.

PART III

TANGIBLE RESOLUTIONS

CHAPTER 10

A PAINFUL PILL TO SWALLOW

"Doctor...why did he die?"

A common, albeit unfortunate, question asked by the granddaughter of a patient in the ICU.

As a twenty-year-old college student, I struggled with this question.

"I am so sorry for your loss. Your grandfather had a heart attack, among the most severe I have encountered."

After seeing the patient, the doctor told me the answer was much more complex than that. He told me in medical school, they do not teach that being unable to afford vital drugs can be a cause of death. Apparently, a patient's inability to afford medications is not allowed to be written on death certificates.

In this patient's case, it was apparent—the most obvious cause of death was *inability to pay*. This patient had been at another hospital week prior to his death. The patient had come to the hospital with the chief complaint of chest pain. The doctor prescribed the patient the necessary medications as a heart attack seemed to be the likely case. A cardiac catheterization, in which a catheter is inserted into either a vein or an artery and threaded through blood vessels leading to the heart, was performed, and the patient was relieved as a result. The patient was counseled on the importance of the medications prescribed and how important it was to adhere to them.

When the patient went to his local pharmacy, he found out that despite his insurance, *one* medication would cost him over $200 every month. Unfortunately, despite having the necessary $200 in the bank, this patient had several grandchildren to take care of. Hence, the patient decided *why not do without for some days and fill the prescription every few days.*

Those few days were enough to cause the patient to have a heart attack—one that took his life and changed the life of his grandchildren.

HYPERTENSION AND QUALITY OF CARE
This patient did not just *fall through the cracks* of our currently broken healthcare system. He was a victim of the exorbitantly expensive medication costs we, as patients, are subject to by pharmaceutical companies focused on generating the most profit.

And the worst part of this? *His story is not unique.* In fact, about 25 percent of patients in the United States state that they have trouble paying for their prescribed medications.[322] Moreover, about 80 percent of US patients want governmental regulation of pharmaceutical companies.[323] However, the federal government is controlled by the Pharmaceutical Research and Manufacturers of America (PhRMA), which is the largest lobbying body that embodies the preferences of pharmaceutical companies in DC.[324] It is not hard to understand why the federal government is not as privy to reform as the vast majority of American patients.

We, as American patients, pay approximately four times as much for medications as patients in other countries.[325] This is just an average.[326] In extreme cases, Americans pay more than sixty times as much for the same medication.[327]

Currently, the pharmaceutical industry tries to justify this by stating that rebates offered are much greater, and as a result the net price for a drug is comparable in the United States and other countries. However, this is not the case. A simple comparison

---

322 "Poll: Nearly 1 in 4 Americans Taking Prescription Drugs Say It's Difficult to Afford Their Medicines, including Larger Shares Among Those with Health Issues, with Low Incomes and Nearing Medicare Age," *KFF,* March 1, 2019.

323 Ibid.

324 "Poll: Nearly 1 in 4 Americans Taking Prescription Drugs Say It's Difficult to Afford Their Medicines, including Larger Shares Among Those with Health Issues, with Low Incomes and Nearing Medicare Age," *KFF,* March 1, 2019.

325 Ibid.

326 "Poll: Nearly 1 in 4 Americans Taking Prescription Drugs Say It's Difficult to Afford Their Medicines, including Larger Shares Among Those with Health Issues, with Low Incomes and Nearing Medicare Age," *KFF,* March 1, 2019.

327 Ibid.

between the United States and Germany rebate rates by the Congressional Budget Office in 2019 showed that in Germany, the rebate rates are around 9 percent on average.[328] The rebate rates in the United States would have to be around 73 percent on average to have the US net prices match with other countries looked at in the study.[329] Were the United States to have the same drug prices, on average, as other countries, the country could save nearly $50 billion every year on just Medicare Part D.[330]

By all measures, the US pharmaceutical industry has American consumers paying far more than those in other countries.

Dr. Thomas R. Frieden, president and CEO of Resolve to Save Lives (RTSL), led a study in 2019 on his experience with the Resolve to Save Lives hypertension management program, which worked with the WHO.[331]

High blood pressure takes more lives than all of the currently known infectious diseases combined and is also the leading cause of death.[332] However, hypertension is only controlled with medications by fewer than 15 percent of the population with hypertension.[333]

---

328 "Major Recurring Reports," *Congressional Budget Office*.

329 Ibid.

330 "Major Recurring Reports," *Congressional Budget Office*.

331 Thomas R. Frieden, Cherian V. Varghese, Sandeep P. Kishore, Norman R.C. Campbell, Andrew E. Moran, Raj Padwal, and Marc G. Jaffe. "Scaling up effective treatment of hypertension—A pathfinder for universal health coverage," *The Journal of Clinical Hypertension 21*, no. 10, (September 23, 2019).

332 Ibid.

333 Thomas R. Frieden, Cherian V. Varghese, Sandeep P. Kishore, Norman R.C. Campbell, Andrew E. Moran, Raj Padwal, and Marc G. Jaffe. "Scaling up effective treatment of hypertension—A pathfinder for universal health coverage," *The Journal of Clinical Hypertension 21*, no. 10, (September 23, 2019).

Improvements in the management of hypertension can save more than 100 million lives globally within the next thirty years.[334]

Resolve To Save Lives is an initiative focused on the expansion of controlling hypertension.[335] According to the WHO, there are five necessary criteria that need to be met in order for effective controlling of hypertension:[336]

1. Dosage-specific treatment

2. Patient-centric care

3. Team-centric care

4. Quality improvement

5. Quality assurance

By instituting pragmatic protocols, hypertension rates can be controlled by lowering the cost of associated treatment, maintaining a high quality of care, and reducing variability.[337]

---

334 Ibid.

335 Thomas R. Frieden, Cherian V. Varghese, Sandeep P. Kishore, Norman R.C. Campbell, Andrew E. Moran, Raj Padwal, and Marc G. Jaffe. "Scaling up effective treatment of hypertension—A pathfinder for universal health coverage," *The Journal of Clinical Hypertension* 21, no. 10, (September 23, 2019).

336 Ibid.

337 Thomas R. Frieden, Cherian V. Varghese, Sandeep P. Kishore, Norman R.C. Campbell, Andrew E. Moran, Raj Padwal, and Marc G. Jaffe. "Scaling up effective treatment of hypertension—A pathfinder for universal health coverage," *The Journal of Clinical Hypertension* 21, no. 10, (September 23, 2019).

Studying the control rates of hypertension can serve as a benchmark for how effective a particular healthcare system is running and can also provide an indication of whether or not the accessibility to healthcare is being adequately met. One of the Sustainable Development Goals (SDG) established by the United Nations is to reduce by one-third the premature mortality rates from noncommunicable diseases by the year 2030.[338] By addressing hypertension, various interconnected aspects of primary care can be addressed to increase access to quality healthcare.[339]

THE MICROSOFT VS. LICENSING APPROACH TO REDUCING PHARMACEUTICAL PRICING

Closing the door to the blistering Texan heat, I was relieved to hear my grandma's voice calling me to taste refreshing ice-bathed custard. Now, to be completely honest, I may have eaten more than my fair share. As a matter of habit, my grandma directed me to swallow my vitamins.

Slurping a tablet down your throat, have you ever wondered why this tiny pill is so expensive? Consider this: a five-hundred-milligram Tylenol tablet costs eight dollars.[340]

Currently, there is an evident need to address the opacity in drug prices, which creates a lot of uncertainty in accessibility.

---

338 Ibid.

339 Thomas R. Frieden, Cherian V. Varghese, Sandeep P. Kishore, Norman R.C. Campbell, Andrew E. Moran, Raj Padwal, and Marc G. Jaffe. "Scaling up effective treatment of hypertension—A pathfinder for universal health coverage," *The Journal of Clinical Hypertension 21*, no. 10, (September 23, 2019).

340 "Pharbetol Extra Strength Coupons & Prices," *SingleCare*.

In the consideration of a solution, the following criteria need to be addressed:

- Increased simplicity in calculating the cost of drugs.

- Cost should be phased through the duration of drug benefit rather than solely at time of intervention.

  - This can enable patients to evaluate the effectiveness of a drug through the entirety of the intervention process. As a result, pricing will be based far more on the value rather than the design of the drug.

- The price of drugs should be directly linked to the *value* delivered by a particular drug.

- There should be decreased variability in drug costs based on a patient's physique and increased predictability of the overall price impact for patients.

A license model can be adapted from companies such as Microsoft. When applied to the healthcare system, payers provide a monthly fee for each patient for using that drug's intellectual property, instead of how much of the drug was used.

Through this approach, there is a greater focus on outcomes. Moreover, this would allow for allaying of the obstacles that come with deferred benefits and high costs.

The vast majority of the *value* that comes from an innovative drug is in the intellectual property, instead of a value being tied specifically to certain compounds.[341]

An approach similar to Microsoft can be adopted where drugs are paid for based on health outcomes and hence *value* would be the main determinator as a result.

Below is a chart summarizing the pros and cons of using a Microsoft-esque approach to pharmaceutical pricing:

Pros	Cons
Increased certainty of pricing; lower upfront cost	Current healthcare system is not well suited for this approach
Value-based	Ease of misuse of drugs
Able to protect both the licensee and licensor	Increased cost burden for patients for prolonged duration
Tiered pricing based on GDP, the total market or monetary value of all the finished goods and services produced within a country in a specific time frame	Risky and thus unlikely to be considered by the pharmaceutical industry

The license approach will allow for increased *certainty* and will reduce the budget impact through availability of options for covering combination protocols.

---

341 Emily H. Jung, Alfred Engelberg, and Aaron S. Kesselheim, "Do large pharma companies provide drug development innovation? Our analysis says no," *Statnews*, December 10, 2019.

Another approach is pricing based on related diseases.

Below is a chart summarizing the pros and cons of grouping pharmaceuticals in terms of related diseases:

Pros	Cons
Increased certainty of budget impact	Current healthcare system is not well suited for this approach
Value-based	Ease of misuse of drugs
Works for both single-agent and combination protocols	Time-consuming—however, this can be mitigated through interim measures such as Q codes (The Q codes are used to identify services not given in a CPT code, such as drugs, biologicals, and other types of medical equipment or services, and which are not identified by national Level II codes). *NOTE: Current Procedural Terminology (CPT) is a medical code set that is used to report medical, surgical, and diagnostic procedures and services to entities such as physicians, health insurance companies, and accreditation organizations.*
No discrimination against patients with a high BMI (Body mass index, a value derived from the mass and height of a person)	A lot of variation in disease-related groups across healthcare systems

Moreover, yet another approach can be the securitizing of credit facilities to debt instruments that can be traded.

A drug known as Erlotinib works for both pancreatic and lung cancer.[342] Data analysis shows that Erlotinib prolongs life by several months for a patient with lung cancer.[343] However, it only prolongs life by a couple of weeks for pancreatic cancer.[344] Is it just to have no difference in pricing despite value differences? This drug is a prime example of the urgency to change the way drug pricing is done.

There are, however, several challenges that come with these propositions. Namely, these are untested. Top priority should be assigned to the benefits obtained by the patient as measured through *value*. Another challenge is the assignment of the criterion associated with outcome levels of a certain disease. With a change in drug pricing, it is imperative there is proper monitoring of each drug. The utility of tracking mechanisms may be required to avoid misuse.

In adopting these propositions, another issue is adapting to a system that holds no value for a vial. One mechanism to deal with this involves the manufacturer having the ownership of a drug until the distribution phase.

A FREE-MARKET APPROACH

Let us take, for instance, a healthcare system having better outcomes than the United States *and* being 75 percent

---

342 Jason Fernando, "Gross Domestic Product (GDP)," *Investopedia*, November 13, 2020.

343 Lori-Lynne A. Webb, "Note similarities and differences between HCPCS, CPT codes," *HCPRO*, September 5, 2012.

344 Kristen Lee, "Current Procedural Terminology (CPT) Code," *SearchHealthIT*, June 2015.

cheaper.[345] This is the reality in Singapore.[346] Now, it was not always like this. A few decades back, Singapore had a significantly worse healthcare system, but it is now among the world's finest.

The conclusion? A capitalistic system *with* a safety net feature does indeed work.

By having a third-party system in the United States, among the patients, healthcare providers, and the insurance companies, the drivers are, as a result, the third party. Consequently, hospitals are aware their revenue is based far more on their negotiation with insurance companies instead of the *value* they provide for patients.

Singapore has a two-party system.[347] Adapting the mindset that the consumer should be in control of the market, the patient controls the healthcare market in Singapore.[348] The patients pay part of their earnings into essentially a health savings account (HSA).[349] The patients also own the assets.[350] The patients

---

345 Naureen Starling, John Neoptolemos, and David Cunningham, "Role of erlotinib in the management of pancreatic cancer," *Dovepress Therapeutics and Clinical Risk Management* 2, no. 4, December 2006.

346 Ibid.

347 Naureen Starling, John Neoptolemos, and David Cunningham, "Role of erlotinib in the management of pancreatic cancer," *Dovepress Therapeutics and Clinical Risk Management* 2, no. 4, December 2006.

348 Roosa Tikkanen, Robin Osborn, Elias Mossialos, Ana Djordjevic, George A. Wharton, "International Health Care System Profiles Singapore," *The Commonwealth Fund*, June 5, 2020.

349 Ibid.

350 Roosa Tikkanen, Robin Osborn, Elias Mossialos, Ana Djordjevic, George A. Wharton, "International Health Care System Profiles Singapore," *The Commonwealth Fund*, June 5, 2020.

pay premiums for insurance for covering the very expensive treatments *and* routine costs.[351] The remainder in the HSA stays in the account and can be saved for future expenses.[352]

Singapore also mandates price transparency.[353] Due to this, surprise medical billing is out of the question.[354] The hospitals compete for the patient, and that competition drives prices down.[355] The patient has the choice of getting better amenities, but the quality of care remains the same regardless of the patient's socioeconomic status.[356] In the United States, patients need to spend a significant amount of time before they can begin to discern the differences in the prices between different pharmaceutical medications.[357]

Take, for instance, a doctor who had a secretary to take care of scheduling his appointments, another staff member to take care of regular practice assignments, and two other staff members to work with insurance companies. On the other side of the table, there are at minimum two more people. This means there are at least five staff members per provider.

---

351 Ibid.

352 Roosa Tikkanen, Robin Osborn, Elias Mossialos, Ana Djordjevic, George A. Wharton, "International Health Care System Profiles Singapore," *The Commonwealth Fund*, June 5, 2020.

353 Ibid.

354 Roosa Tikkanen, Robin Osborn, Elias Mossialos, Ana Djordjevic, George A. Wharton, "International Health Care System Profiles Singapore," *The Commonwealth Fund*, June 5, 2020.

355 Ibid.

356 Roosa Tikkanen, Robin Osborn, Elias Mossialos, Ana Djordjevic, George A. Wharton, "International Health Care System Profiles Singapore," *The Commonwealth Fund*, June 5, 2020.

357 Ibid.

Moreover, insurance companies profit off of the number of claims filed. Clearly, this is not an excellent strategy to control expenses.

In Singapore, any drug is deemed *good*, so long as approval from major drug regulatory agencies has been done.[358] One of the major differences between the United States and Singapore in this regard is the United States requires the drug be both *safe* and *efficacious*.[359] In Singapore, the idea is that market competition will take care of the *efficacious* criteria and thus there should be no need to have a criterion in the regulatory process.[360] Following suit of this "do no harm" methodology is much less expensive, and the quality level is not lower.[361] The consequential expense from the US approach to drug regulation by the FDA has prevented accessibility to drugs for many who would be able to otherwise afford that drug.[362]

Clearly, a free-market approach would work in the United States. In fact, elective surgeries not covered by insurance are an excellent example of this. Both demand and outcomes have improved. Once accounting for inflation, the prices have declined as well.

---

358 Roosa Tikkanen, Robin Osborn, Elias Mossialos, Ana Djordjevic, George A. Wharton, "International Health Care System Profiles Singapore," *The Commonwealth Fund*, June 5, 2020.

359 Ibid.

360 Roosa Tikkanen, Robin Osborn, Elias Mossialos, Ana Djordjevic, George A. Wharton, "International Health Care System Profiles Singapore," *The Commonwealth Fund*, June 5, 2020.

361 Ibid.

362 Roosa Tikkanen, Robin Osborn, Elias Mossialos, Ana Djordjevic, George A. Wharton, "International Health Care System Profiles Singapore," *The Commonwealth Fund*, June 5, 2020.

Hence, the approach to reducing drug pricing is critical and well overdue. An approach that focuses first and foremost on *value* and, in doing so, emphasizes ease of access in a sustainable manner is of utmost importance.

CONCLUSION
- Studying the control rates of hypertension can serve as a benchmark for how effective a particular healthcare system is running and can also provide an indication of whether or not the accessibility to healthcare is being adequately met. By addressing hypertension, various interconnected aspects of primary care can be addressed to increase access to quality healthcare.

- Approaches to reducing exorbitant pharmaceutical pricing:

  - A license model can be adapted from companies such as Microsoft (when applied to the healthcare system, payers provide a monthly fee for each patient for using that drug's intellectual property, instead of how much of the drug was used);

  - Pricing based on related diseases; and

  - The securitizing of credit facilities to debt instruments that can be traded.

- A capitalistic system *with* a safety net feature does indeed work.

CHAPTER 11

A PRIMER ON HEALTH INSURANCE

CARDIOLOGIST VISIT—MALPRACTICE CASE

A thirty-one-year-old came to visit his cardiologist with the chief complaint of chest pain. Having noticed through the patient's chart a risk for coronary disease, the cardiologist ordered a nuclear stress exam a week from the visit.

On the day prior to the nuclear stress exam, the patient had excessive exertion, and during this period, the patient passed away. Expectedly, the patient's family sued the cardiologist since there were no explicit instructions given to the patient and the patient's family on avoiding excess exertion.

When the patient's family and the cardiologist arrived in court, the cardiologist argued the patient was indeed instructed to avoid excess exertion until the nuclear stress exam was administered. The court ruled 40 percent of the liability fell on the patient, and the rest fell on the cardiologist. With consideration of the fact that the cardiologist had malpractice insurance coverage for the normal $1 million, the cardiologist would be left $2 million short.

Juries are indeed unpredictable. Provided the plaintiff is deemed victorious, there is a considerable chance the patient's family would receive several millions. How might medical providers protect themselves against such a financially detrimental situation when the alternative is to provide the carrier the ability to pay an amount in addition to the policy limits?

Currently, this is done through what is known as a high/low agreement, in which the provider is able to stand in court and possibly be vindicated as *not liable*, without the carrier paying the plaintiff an amount in addition to the policy limits.[363] In such an agreement, a provider might be concerned an injured patient will invoke an emotional response from the jury, particularly in finance discussions. Similarly, an impoverished individual may generate some sympathy. These are some cases in which the judgments can be in the millions and potentially bankrupt a primary care physician.

Conversely, a plaintiff may support the provider, and the plaintiff may receive nothing in compensation.

By having a contract-based high/low agreement between the involved parties, a compromise can be reached. For instance, if the settlements are $100,000 and $1 million, then there are two possible scenarios. First, the jury may hold the provider liable for a *high* value, in which case the provider would have

---

363 B. Sonny Bal, "An Introduction to Medical Malpractice in the United States," *Clinical Orthopaedics and Related Research* 467, no.2, (November 26, 2008).

to pay the *high* value of $1 million. Second, the jury may hold the provider not liable, and in this case the provider would have to pay the *low* value of $100,000.

In this particular case, there was no material proof to suggest whether or not the cardiologist had given proper instructions to avoid exertion. As such, utilizing the high/low strategy might have served to lower the risk for the cardiologist.

MALPRACTICE INSURANCE COVERAGE

The mosaic of affirmed rules and regulations forming medical malpractice is based on three main fundamentals: liability, providing medical care, and tort law, an area of law that protects people from others' negligent actions.[364]

A current source of frustration is that there are different premises for health and liability insurance. Healthcare has evolved to become much more regulated over the past few decades. Through employer insurance coverage, there has been considerable success. However, third-party liability coverage, focused exclusively on protecting clients from litigation costs, has experienced insufficient success.

Malpractice insurance coverage for providers is fixated in the midst of typical negligence and preindustrial healthcare.[365] Should a provider not meet the standard of care, he or she would be liable for civil litigation. Cases involving

---

364 Ibid.

365 B. Sonny Bal, "An Introduction to Medical Malpractice in the United States," *Clinical Orthopaedics and Related Research* 467, no.2, (November 26, 2008).

significant injury typically take more than five years for resolution.[366] Oftentimes, there is hidden information from patients and their families, quality feedback is biased as higher-than-actual ratings are often recorded, and compensation is late consistently.

How is it that what seemed like a reasonable mechanism for protecting a provider is counterproductive? Moreover, why are liability insurances so affected by accessibility crises? A look from the 1960s provides some answers.

In the 1960s, there were several medical societies that protected clients from malpractice claims through a fraternal pooled resource model.[367] More often than not, litigation was focused on more reputed providers.[368] The original intent of malpractice defense was for provider accountability. Through the 1960s, there was increased liberalization of laws. Generally, there was a rise in litigation.[369] However, there was a lower claim frequency when compared to other retails such as automobiles.[370] The financial expenses were still higher in healthcare, despite this.[371] Due to these factors, insurers faced

---

366 Ibid.

367 B. Sonny Bal, "An Introduction to Medical Malpractice in the United States," *Clinical Orthopaedics and Related Research* 467, no.2, (November 26, 2008).

368 Ibid.

369 B. Sonny Bal, "An Introduction to Medical Malpractice in the United States," *Clinical Orthopaedics and Related Research* 467, no.2, (November 26, 2008).

370 Ibid.

371 B. Sonny Bal, "An Introduction to Medical Malpractice in the United States," *Clinical Orthopaedics and Related Research* 467, no.2, (November 26, 2008).

difficulty in accurate price coverage.[372] This issue was further attenuated by jury generosity in assessing premiums.[373]

In the 1970s, malpractice insurance became much more difficult for commercial insurance companies.[374] In 1975, there was a fragile investment climate due to the oil-shock recession.[375] Due to this, claims rose in both severity and in number.[376] As a result, a large portion of medical providers in the United States were left without malpractice insurance coverage.[377]

Legislatures responded through tort reform.[378] One example of this was the Medical Injury Compensation Reform Act by the state of California (MICRA).[379] MICRA was focused on restoring the viability of private liability insurance.[380] Moreover, there were several medical societies focused on

---

372 Ibid.

373 B. Sonny Bal, "An Introduction to Medical Malpractice in the United States," *Clinical Orthopaedics and Related Research* 467, no.2, (November 26, 2008).

374 Ibid.

375 B. Sonny Bal, "An Introduction to Medical Malpractice in the United States," *Clinical Orthopaedics and Related Research* 467, no.2, (November 26, 2008).

376 Ibid.

377 B. Sonny Bal, "An Introduction to Medical Malpractice in the United States," *Clinical Orthopaedics and Related Research* 467, no.2, (November 26, 2008).

378 Ibid.

379 B. Sonny Bal, "An Introduction to Medical Malpractice in the United States," *Clinical Orthopaedics and Related Research* 467, no.2, (November 26, 2008).

380 Ibid.

chartering mutual carriers.[381] Additional reforms included guaranty funds and joint underwriting associations (JUAs).[382] In brief, guaranty funds are designed to protect policyholders when an insurance company defaults on benefit payments or is insolvent.[383] JUAs involve insurers joining together to provide coverage for a certain risk when it is difficult to obtain coverage in the regular market.[384]

During the 1980s, the liability insurance crisis brought rising premiums and unavailability of coverage.[385] The provider-sponsored carriers were focused on their main customers, and with the political settlements and distribution of organization power to determine policies of the 1970s likely to persist, there were considerable legal risks arising.[386] A nadir of profitability became a marker of the insurance cycle due to much lower interest rates, which resulted in lower investment income, causing there to be increased pressure on premium levels.[387] Occurrence and claims-made policies are two forms

---

381 B. Sonny Bal, "An Introduction to Medical Malpractice in the United States," *Clinical Orthopaedics and Related Research* 467, no.2, (November 26, 2008).

382 Ibid.

383 B. Sonny Bal, "An Introduction to Medical Malpractice in the United States," *Clinical Orthopaedics and Related Research* 467, no.2, (November 26, 2008).

384 Ibid.

385 B. Sonny Bal, "An Introduction to Medical Malpractice in the United States," *Clinical Orthopaedics and Related Research* 467, no.2, (November 26, 2008).

386 B. Sonny Bal, "An Introduction to Medical Malpractice in the United States," *Clinical Orthopaedics and Related Research* 467, no.2, (November 26, 2008).

387 Ibid.

of insurance coverage.[388] Occurrence policies cover losses within a certain time interval, regardless of when an incident was reported.[389] Claims-made policies cover incidents reported during the active policy period and occur after a policy's retroactive start date.[390] The carriers continued the transition from occurrence policies to a claims-made policy; this allowed for no price uncertainty to be associated with the sentiments of the jury through the duration when care was rendered and when the claim was filed.[391]

Starting in the 1990s to the current time, malpractice insurance has grown to become much worse than prior times, especially so in specialties such as surgery and emergency medicine.[392] Many carriers opted for competing in different geographical markets through lower premiums and loosening the JUA underwriting criteria.[393] Hence, claims have risen in both number and severity.[394] Moreover, with global insurance shocks involving catastrophes such as terrorist attacks, there

---

388 B. Sonny Bal, "An Introduction to Medical Malpractice in the United States," *Clinical Orthopaedics and Related Research* 467, no.2, (November 26, 2008).

389 Ibid.

390 B. Sonny Bal, "An Introduction to Medical Malpractice in the United States," *Clinical Orthopaedics and Related Research* 467, no.2, (November 26, 2008).

391 Ibid.

392 B. Sonny Bal, "An Introduction to Medical Malpractice in the United States," *Clinical Orthopaedics and Related Research* 467, no.2, (November 26, 2008).

393 Ibid.

394 B. Sonny Bal, "An Introduction to Medical Malpractice in the United States," *Clinical Orthopaedics and Related Research* 467, no.2, (November 26, 2008).

is scarce capital, especially within the realm of malpractice insurance for providers.[395] These skyrocketing reinsurance costs are impacting the main carriers and hospitals. Moreover, price shocks, whereby commodity prices change significantly within a short period of time, are especially evident in tight markets, a trading environment where the pricing difference between the best bid and the offer is small, and as a result the market becomes more expensive and less reliable, with significantly worse case projections.[396]

A focus on current malpractice reform is merely a rallying cry among the business community and consumer interests over personal injury litigation on the social fabric. No side has a genuine interest in focusing on the subtleties of medical malpractice insurance coverage since it defies the expression of a clean narrative in regards on the litigation enterprise. Moreover, medical malpractice insurers seldom articulate a critical need for innovation in managing liability risk; rather, they assert parochial positions against the need for incurring liability risk and focused on reverberation of the rhetoric, either in favor of or against the litigation enterprise, of their medical providers (their sponsors) and protection of their narrow risks.[397]

The current state of malpractice medical insurance is the reflection of the success of contemporary healthcare, *not* the failure. Medicine is not a charitable enterprise whereby patients paying for their healthcare and insurance are conditioned to expect

---

395 Ibid.

396 B. Sonny Bal, "An Introduction to Medical Malpractice in the United States," *Clinical Orthopaedics and Related Research* 467, no.2, (November 26, 2008).

397 Ibid.

success, attributing subpar results to misconduct. For risks of such a magnitude to be supported by the malpractice medical insurance of a provider, there need to be large risk pools, and there are often collateral sources of payments.

Advances in medicine have allowed for there to be increased sensitivity to medical errors. With widespread medical errors, there is social importance. Tort litigation is not equipped to address this concern since liability insurers are focused on claim deterrence and error contestation.

SOLUTIONS

There needs to be a focus on improving the integration of liability coverage into the commercial and regulatory frame of delivering healthcare.

Within the private sector during the 1970s, commercial insurers who were not working closely with healthcare lost interest in medical malpractice insurance and were instead replaced by providers.[398] A lot of these entities became businesses to parallel the reorientation for government marketing.[399] At the same time, industrialization has caused a shift toward other coverage forms such as self-insurance and risk retention, in an effort to align risk management with management among discrete institutions.[400]

---

398 B. Sonny Bal, "An Introduction to Medical Malpractice in the United States," *Clinical Orthopaedics and Related Research* 467, no.2, (November 26, 2008).

399 Ibid.

400 B. Sonny Bal, "An Introduction to Medical Malpractice in the United States," *Clinical Orthopaedics and Related Research* 467, no.2, (November 26, 2008).

Mutual carriers are focused on the medical malpractice market and thus are relatively unaffected by the insurance cycle, yet they are not diversified well and have subpar capital. Coverage connected to medical institutions look favorable, especially if providers and the medical institution have a common interest financially to decrease the liability risk across the clinical services offered. Medical institutional costs are based on risk, ensuring liability has a deterrent effect regardless of the insurance cycle.[401] There is also a more equal distribution of liability costs across specialists, in addition to the revenue streams.[402] Medical institutions also have the advantage of crafting other options for malpractice litigation to decrease the volatility of liability costs.[403]

The main regulators of health insurance come from the state government. Solvency can be maintained and marketing coverage can be monitored to allow for policymakers to receive the benefits from their premium contributions.[404] State governments should focus on economic downturns in order to protect against the rising insurance premiums.[405] At the peak of the insurance cycle, insurers can reduce prices, and this may backfire due to changing economic conditions.[406]

---

401 Ibid.

402 B. Sonny Bal, "An Introduction to Medical Malpractice in the United States," *Clinical Orthopaedics and Related Research* 467, no.2, (November 26, 2008).

403 Ibid.

404 B. Sonny Bal, "An Introduction to Medical Malpractice in the United States," *Clinical Orthopaedics and Related Research* 467, no.2, (November 26, 2008).

405 Ibid.

406 B. Sonny Bal, "An Introduction to Medical Malpractice in the United States," Clinical Orthopaedics and Related Research 467, no.2, (November 26, 2008).

Regulation of rates can decrease responsiveness to the preferences of patients to lower premiums.[407] This is commonly seen for auto insurance.

Through the integration of medical malpractice insurance, the rate at which injuries are recognized needs to be increased and can be through a shift from third-party to first-party liability coverage and linking quality of care with risk management at the medical institutional level.

Moreover, there needs to be a reconsideration of risk pooling. Currently, JUAs are essentially irrelevant to high-quality care accessibility. Risk pooling can be reconsidered by distributing liability costs to a more equitable distribution among providers through diversified risk pooling, increased monitoring of health insurance reimbursements, and avoiding subrogation claims against those who defend medical malpractice.[408]

There are three main reasons why a federal presence in medical malpractice insurance coverage is necessary. Firstly, a significant precipitant of the current issue surrounding medical liability coverage is the cost of reinsurance. Only the federal government has the fiscal capability to allow for substitution of public reinsurance with private reinsurance. This could potentially reduce the financial issues on providers and hospitals.

Secondly, there are many approaches to increasing coverage being established at the institutional level instead of the

---

407 Ibid.

408 B. Sonny Bal, "An Introduction to Medical Malpractice in the United States," *Clinical Orthopaedics and Related Research* 467, no.2, (November 26, 2008).

corporate level, which is what the state regulators are most accustomed to. Since the 1980s, the federal government has been the main regulator of risk-retention groups and has been able to leverage this to aid providers to develop even more efficient risk-bearing strategies.[409]

Lastly, the funding responsibility for progress in benefit distribution has shifted from the state government to the federal government.

There are two main ways through which federal government intervention can be implemented. The first approach is where the federal government can support the state government–based medical malpractice reform to replace the litigation with a system that is more rational in reducing the rates of injury and appropriate compensation.

The second approach is where the federal government devises a restructuring of the medical malpractice claims that involve Medicaid and Medicare patients. This standard can be applied to the entire healthcare system. The most effective means of medical malpractice insurance to be on the federal policy agenda is where Medicare takes ownership. For instance, Medicare-led reform could utilize the already established admin adjudication to link the compensation of injuries that are preventable to other initiatives to improve quality.

---

409 Ibid.

CONCLUSION

- The mosaic of affirmed rules and regulations forming medical malpractice is based on three main fundamentals: liability, providing medical care, and tort law.

- The current state of malpractice medical insurance is the reflection of the success of contemporary healthcare, *not* the failure.

- There needs to be a focus on improving the integration of liability coverage into the commercial and regulatory frame of delivering healthcare.

- Through the integration of medical malpractice insurance, the rate at which injuries are recognized needs to be increased and can be through a shift from third-party to first-party liability coverage and linking quality of care with risk management at the medical institutional level.

- Risk pooling can be reconsidered by distributing liability costs to a more equitable distribution among providers through diversified risk pooling, increased monitoring of health insurance reimbursements, and avoiding subrogation claims against those who defend medical malpractice.

- Federal intervention:

  – The federal government can support the state government–based medical malpractice reform to replace litigation with a system that is more rational in reducing the rates of injury and appropriate compensation.

- The federal government can devise a restructuring of the medical malpractice claims that involve Medicaid and Medicare patients.

CHAPTER 12

THE AFFORDABILITY SCALE

During an interview with Dr. Paul B. Rothman, CEO of Johns Hopkins Medicine, he outlines the importance of personalized medical care that can be aided through AI.

Dr. Rothman states he was not expecting the rate of viral spread to be as fast as it was. Interestingly, when discussing how Johns Hopkins responded to COVID-19, Dr. Rothman shares the first pertinent response was to focus as much on COVID-19 cases as possible. Moreover, there was an increase in the usage of telemedicine because it was covered by several insurance companies. In addition, telemedicine is viewed as a more efficient means of working with patients. Of course, it was not a total shift to telemedicine, but a significant portion of the medical care process incorporated telemedicine to a greater degree when compared to the pre-COVID-19 era.

When asked about how the United States has handled the COVID-19 pandemic compared to other countries, Dr.

Rothman shared that the variance in responses was due to states playing a far greater role in how COVID-19 was dealt with.

Dr. Rothman also shared that COVID-19 is particularly difficult for the world to deal with because there is a very long pre-symptomatic period. This means that days can go by, and there are likely to be no symptoms. This means a very fast spread rate.

Moreover, an interesting question that Johns Hopkins Medicine has been examining, per Dr. Rothman, is understanding how and why it is that certain populations are more predisposed to COVID-19's severe impact. AI is playing an important role in examining this question.

In recent years, there have been significant improvements in value-based healthcare through innovative reimbursement systems. The main focus here has been on high levels of the healthcare providers' performance and low levels of cost. However, there has been a lack thereof. One possible solution is to institute a tool that can assist all parties involved in a patient's care, including the patient, so those involved have a deep understanding of the patient's share of the cost and how much the patient can afford.

There is an increasing need for healthcare cost information. In 2011, 26.3 percent of adults between the ages of eighteen and sixty-four had high-deductible health plans, and in 2016 this rose to 39.3 percent.[410] The next frontier of value is healthcare affordability for patients.

---

[410] Robin A. Cohen and Emily P. Zammitti, "High-deductible Health Plan Enrollment Among Adults Aged 18-64 With Employment-based Insurance Coverage," *Centers for Disease Control and Prevention*, August 2018.

A Gallup poll done in 2018 showed that approximately 30 percent of Americans delay seeing the doctor due to fear of costs.[411] This number rose from 2004, when it was 24 percent.[412] This implies patients from a low socioeconomic status have limited access to care. There are very few payers in the US healthcare system that are involved in creating incentives, whether this be financial or intrinsic, to benefit patients from low socioeconomic backgrounds. According to a study in 2003, 63 percent of patients want to discuss their out-of-pocket payments with their healthcare provider and 79 percent of healthcare providers also want to discuss such payments.[413] However, in reality only 15 percent of patients and 35 percent of healthcare providers actually reported having a conversation on out-of-pocket payments.[414] This may be because patients are under the assumption that out-of-pocket payments are set in stone and there are no opportunities to receive affordable, quality care.

According to the Center for Medicare and Medicaid Services, hospitals are required to share their standard rates online.[415] However, this is quite misleading. Most hospitals post the information using medical terminology and abbreviations that most patients are not familiar with. Moreover, these standard rates do not account for the financial obligation

---

411 Lydia Saad, "More Americans Delaying Medical Treatment Due to Cost," *Gallup*, December 9, 2019.

412 Ibid.

413 Lydia Saad, "More Americans Delaying Medical Treatment Due to Cost," *Gallup*, December 9, 2019.

414 Ibid.

415 Lydia Saad, "More Americans Delaying Medical Treatment Due to Cost," *Gallup*, December 9, 2019.

of patients. By virtue, healthcare systems are positioned to direct affordability campaigns.

In today's competitive landscape, affordability can be a means of differentiation. Currently, there is no standard scale for defining an affordability scale for patients. Through the utilization of an affordability scale, this paradigm would be enhanced and would be based on these components. First, providers would address affordability issues more effectively due to ease of transparency. Second, healthcare delivery (medical care, therapeutic and diagnostic intervention, and pharmaceutical care) would be provided at a high quality but at lower costs. Thirdly, there would be transparency of out-of-pocket payments. Lastly, various avenues would be open to address issues of affordability.

Providers can address affordability issues more effectively through three main measures. Providers can be trained on financial conversations, resources can be developed to address affordability issues, and accountability at all levels of care can be established.

Transparency of out-of-pocket payments can be addressed when the patient is provided data about their treatment by the provider, care site, and payer, a company that pays for an administered medical service. This may involve creating strong relationships with payers. Moreover, by designing a strategy to deliver transparent data to providers, accountability can be maintained. This may involve using unblinded data transparency at the training level.

In order to address affordability, support care pathways can be developed. Also, implementing universal screening and high-risk committees to address patient needs can address affordability concerns.

This affordability scale can be used as a standard. By assessing hospitals with the same standard, governing bodies will be able to provide more pertinent information. This standard can be publicized to allow for ease of accessibility to ultimately allow for patients to make informed decisions on where they should seek care.

Currently, there are indices focused on out-of-pocket costs and on insurance. However, through the implementation of an affordability scale, patients will be able to make decisions with a clear understanding of how medical billing is done and moreover will be able to understand how to address situations when patient care is necessary but is very expensive. The current indices are limited in their scope of the health system of use. For instance, they exclude uninsured patients and emphasize aggregate financial cost.

Health systems can allow for actionable out-of-pocket cost information for patients through enhanced data management. This will address the financial opacity to patients. This, by itself, will not resolve affordability in healthcare. However, this is still a necessary step to undertake to enable open conversations between providers, patients, and the rest of the healthcare team.

In order to tackle the issue of healthcare accessibility, it is imperative to have strong relationships with payers, and this needs to be backed with governmental healthcare policies.

The price transparency tool, created by the University of Utah, allows for patients to input information about their copayments and deductibles to yield approximate out-of-pocket costs for typical medical procedures.[416] BlueCross North Carolina provides information for consumers on both cost and quality.[417] BlueCross North Carolina expands partnership with benefit companies using behavioral economics to make patients informed at point of care.[418] If, for example, a consumer chooses a high-quality service at a lower cost, that consumer may receive cash reimbursement. This incentivizes the consumer to be involved in decision making for affordable healthcare, and the savings are shared with the patient. Likewise, payers are also developing value-based insurance to exclude copays so that high-value care is encouraged.

In order to obtain all of the benefits of out-of-pocket cost transparency, it is imperative that providers opt for lower-cost options. CVS has addressed this through electronic health records (EHRs) so that providers have access to member-only pharmacy benefits when prescriptions are given.[419] From the preliminary data obtained, it was determined that nearly half of the providers opted for lower-cost options as a result.[420]

---

416 Ibid.

417 Lydia Saad, "More Americans Delaying Medical Treatment Due to Cost," *Gallup*, December 9, 2019.

418 Ibid.

419 Lydia Saad, "More Americans Delaying Medical Treatment Due to Cost," *Gallup*, December 9, 2019.

420 Ibid.

It is also very important that healthcare systems enable training of providers to deliver affordable care. This can be done through open discussions on costs, data access at point of care, and incorporation in patient care plans. For instance, healthcare teams can inform patients on both the financial and health impacts of deciding on surgical invention in all three phrases—before, during, and after care delivery.

It is imperative for health systems to develop both financial and clinical pathways to increase healthcare affordability for patients. By developing affordability pathways that account for individualized care for patients and affordability screenings, healthcare systems will be able to reduce the financial risk for patients.

At large, financial distress screening is important for addressing affordability since all socioeconomic backgrounds can be at financial risk. Kaiser Permanente, as an example, implemented a financial screening tool to identify community services that will allow for patients to be assisted with financial planning and sociological determinants of health.[421] If a patient screens positive, healthcare teams follow care pathways to address that patient's particular needs through the use of Health Leads, an organization that enables community resources to be identified for addressing sociological determinants of health.[422] For instance, Health Leads may address food insecurity, provide financial counseling, or provide

---

421 Melissa Ritchie, "Kaiser Permanente creates COVID-19 Social Health Playbook," *Kaiser Permanente,* October 13, 2020.

422 Ibid.

assistance with transportation.[423] Doing so enables providers to ensure patients receive access to quality care rapidly.

Situations have varying degrees of complexity. In the more complex situations in which patients require expensive healthcare they are unable to afford, healthcare systems can utilize expert committees consisting of both clinical and financial experts for guidance. This committee may identify which patients could be eligible for programs, internal and external, to help in covering the cost for patients. Moreover, patients can be incorporated into these committees to facilitate their understanding of the financial risks and to discuss possible solutions based on the affordability scale model. In addition, the committee can determine if the healthcare institution could be forgiving of some expenses or at least work with the payers to advocate for patients.

Lastly, healthcare systems can also address system-wide adoption and implementation challenges through a focus on individualized care teams. Organizations can guide patients toward affordable care through networks such as care sites especially focused on affordability. In addition, this network development may involve creating systems for identifying staff trained to deliver more affordable care. As an example, Costs of Care is partnered with Amino, a healthcare start-up in San Francisco, to have *cost conversations*.[424]

---

423 Melissa Ritchie, "Kaiser Permanente creates COVID-19 Social Health Playbook," *Kaiser Permanente*, October 13, 2020.

424 Ibid.

AN ECONOMIST PERSPECTIVE ON THE AFFORDABILITY SCALE

Let us now consider how the US healthcare system would be if it were based on the consensus of economists. In 2018, there was a survey of ASHEcon Membership presented at the American Society of Health Economics.[425]

Health economists, for one, are in strong favor of keeping the Affordable Care Act, specifically citing that the essence of success is the fact that patients pay a fine if they are uninsured.[426] The argument is that, otherwise, patients who signed up for insurance would be disproportionately sicker—making insurance even more expensive.[427] This might ultimately collapse the market.[428] Hence, there is support for an individual mandate.[429] In 2017, tax cuts reduced the penalty for the uninsured to no penalty; however, the marketplaces have generally remained stable.[430] More than three-fourths of health economists believe premiums should not be higher if a patient has genetic defects.[431] Around three-fourths

---

425 Michael A. Morrisey and Kosali Simon, "The Compensation and Productivity of Health Economists: Results of the 2018 Survey of ASHEcon Membership," *ASHEcon* June 24, 2019.

426 Ibid.

427 Michael A. Morrisey and Kosali Simon, "The Compensation and Productivity of Health Economists: Results of the 2018 Survey of ASHEcon Membership," *ASHEcon,* June 24, 2019.

428 Ibid.

429 Michael A. Morrisey and Kosali Simon, "The Compensation and Productivity of Health Economists: Results of the 2018 Survey of ASHEcon Membership," *ASHEcon,* June 24, 2019.

430 Ibid.

431 Michael A. Morrisey and Kosali Simon, "The Compensation and Productivity of Health Economists: Results of the 2018 Survey of ASHEcon Membership," *ASHEcon,* June 24, 2019.

of health economists are fine with charging patients more if they are involved in unhealthy behaviors.[432]

There have been several ideas to cut down costs in Medicaid and Medicare; however, most health economists are in opposition to these suggestions.[433] Approximately 70 percent of health economists opposed the suggestion of converting Medicare into a program that was based partly on income.[434] This would mean that the full Medicare coverage would not be available all those sixty-five years or older, rather only to those who were below a certain income threshold. Another related idea to this is converting Medicare to a voucher-based program, allowing for a set amount for the government to pay for coverage to allow for health plan shopping.[435] Around 60 percent of health economists are in opposition to this idea.[436]

In the study, out of all of the polls, raising the age of the Medicare eligibility criteria was the least opposed.[437] Around 50 percent were in opposition, 25 percent were in support, and 25 percent did not pick a side.[438]

---

432 Ibid.

433 Michael A. Morrisey and Kosali Simon, "The Compensation and Productivity of Health Economists: Results of the 2018 Survey of ASHEcon Membership," *ASHEcon*, June 24, 2019.

434 Ibid.

435 Michael A. Morrisey and Kosali Simon, "The Compensation and Productivity of Health Economists: Results of the 2018 Survey of ASHEcon Membership," *ASHEcon*, June 24, 2019.

436 Ibid.

437 Michael A. Morrisey and Kosali Simon, "The Compensation and Productivity of Health Economists: Results of the 2018 Survey of ASHEcon Membership," *ASHEcon*, June 24, 2019.

438 Ibid.

It may come as a surprise that the economists who are typically in favor of market-based approaches to governmental programs are supportive of the current structure of Medicare. The reality is economists believe market failures are harmful.

Nearly $250 billion in revenue is lost every year due to employer-sponsored health insurance not being taxed.[439] Most of the health economists believe this results in too generous health insurance plans, thereby wasting the healthcare spending.[440] By and large, health economists are staunchly opposed to this large tax break.[441] Health economists are essentially the group in support of such a view.[442]

When discussing health spending, the pharmaceutical industry is of significant relevance. A sizable portion of drug spending ends up as profit for the pharmaceutical companies. A justification for these high profits is that it spurs innovation due to increased investment motivation. Nearly 50 percent of health economists disagree that pharmaceutical company profits are necessary to incentivize investment motivation.[443]

---

439 Michael A. Morrisey and Kosali Simon, "The Compensation and Productivity of Health Economists: Results of the 2018 Survey of ASHEcon Membership," *ASHEcon,* June 24, 2019.

440 Ibid.

441 Michael A. Morrisey and Kosali Simon, "The Compensation and Productivity of Health Economists: Results of the 2018 Survey of ASHEcon Membership," *ASHEcon,* June 24, 2019.

442 Ibid.

443 Michael A. Morrisey and Kosali Simon, "The Compensation and Productivity of Health Economists: Results of the 2018 Survey of ASHEcon Membership," *ASHEcon,* June 24, 2019.

The remaining 50 percent are split nearly equally between affirmation and no opinion.[444]

Nearly all health economists, more than 90 percent, believe that should employers spend less on health insurance, other employee benefits will increase.[445]

In totality, health economists running the healthcare system would not change the system too much, with the exception of a few things.[446] First, Medicaid would not have a work requirement.[447] Second, taxes would increase for employer-based health insurance, in addition to Medicare.[448]

There is no doubt there are iterative developments in the near future. However, providers that embrace and utilize the affordability scale encompassing point-of-care access to actionable patient-centric affordability information and a system-wide commitment to addressing sociological determinants will be better positioned to address the financial toxicity for the patients that they serve.

---

444 Ibid.

445 Michael A. Morrisey and Kosali Simon, "The Compensation and Productivity of Health Economists: Results of the 2018 Survey of ASHEcon Membership," *ASHEcon*, June 24, 2019.

446 Ibid.

447 Michael A. Morrisey and Kosali Simon, "The Compensation and Productivity of Health Economists: Results of the 2018 Survey of ASHEcon Membership," *ASHEcon*, June 24, 2019.

448 Ibid.

CONCLUSION

- The affordability scale:

    - Providers would address affordability issues more effectively due to ease of transparency.

    - Healthcare delivery (medical care, therapeutic and diagnostic intervention, and pharmaceutical care) would be provided at a high quality but at lower costs.

    - There would be transparency of out-of-pocket payments. Lastly, various avenues would be open to address issues of affordability.

CHAPTER 13

WHAT YOU CAN DO TO FIX THE HEALTHCARE SYSTEM AS A PATIENT

It was a quiet spring day. My friend Alex and I were excited for orchestra practice as a concert was coming up. Shortly after lunch, Alex had a fainting spell. When he went to the nurse's office, he explained this was not the first time this had happened. After running some tests, it was concluded Alex had a kidney problem. Much to his surprise, Alex was stuck in half a year of testing to find the diagnosis. As Alex sat in the waiting room in the hospital for an ultrasound, his medical team came in trepidation. One of the physicians in the team finally spoke up—Alex was diagnosed with not just one but two kidney diseases, and he had just a couple of years of life left.

A dark cloud loomed over Alex. He had no idea what had just happened. He was in utter shock. Alex began preparing himself for the short life he had remaining. He then came across a patient with the name Sienna. The two became friends. A few days later, Alex and Sienna headed to the library to gain an understanding of the medical condition Alex had just been diagnosed with. Upon realization that this diagnosis is typically found in elderly patients, Sienna encouraged Alex to become curious about what had happened and become involved in his care process.

This is not to say the medical care team for Alex was poor; it is simply a reflection of the current healthcare system in the United States, which is dependent on hospitals for every medical-related need, specialists for their specialized views, and guesswork—either something works or the patient passes away. Most important of all, it is dependent on patients who take things at face value and never question anything.

Through a shift toward personalized medicine, many of the current problems can be resolved.

Alex told me about Francis, the one who gave him the kidney he was supposed to never get. He then introduced me to a portable ultrasound that could be plugged into his phone. This is a prime example of how personalized medicine can be achieved.

PERSONALIZED MEDICAL CARE
There are three key characteristics necessary for a successful personalized medical system to be implemented.

First, it is important for care to be available everywhere. Since the late 1700s, hospitals have been around in society.[449] It is important

---

449 "History of Hospitals," *PennNursing, University of Pennsylvania.*

to consider alternatives. Hospitals are often not the best option, and many times they are unsafe for the sickest of patients. Alex recollects during his visit getting bedsores—in essence, being sicker due to the environment of the hospital. Through a shift to at-home care as the default system, personalized medical care can be implemented. A patient needs to earn their way up to a level of sickness to be treated in a hospital setting.

With a shift to at-home care, there will be a lot of devices that need to be worked with. This is where the second principle comes in—a solid care network. There is a dire need to go beyond the paradigm of having specialists and shift toward having a multifaceted care team. At best, the current approach with specialists is uncoordinated and at its worst can cost lives. In fact, more than three-fourths of medical errors are due to uncoordinated efforts. Alex recalls during his care, one of the care providers exclaiming that he had a heart problem—putting Alex into a month of further testing only to realize that Alex was provided with different versions of the same drug. Hence, it is important to understand that the patient–doctor relationship is really a relic of the past. The future is on smart care teams with you, the patient, at the center of it.

With care available everywhere and a solid care network, there will be significant improvements to the current system; however, there still remains guesswork. In 1948, randomized clinical trials were developed to allow for effective invention of drugs for treating conditions such as tuberculosis.[450] The problem, however, is these trials are

---

450 Iain Chalmers, "Why the 1948 MRC trial of streptomycin used treatment allocation based on random numbers," *Journal of the Royal Society of Medicine* 104, no. 9, September 2011.

trained to work with populations, not individuals. This is where the guesswork lies. Big data and high-performance computing are some of the means of building predictive individualized algorithms.

Most importantly, it is important for patients to take control of their healthcare to allow for this approach to work in reality. With that said, here are some things you can do to become a proactive patient:

- Inquire with your provider when something does not make sense;

- Communicate on a regular basis with your provider; and

- Create your personal health record.

DISCUSSION ON HEALTH LITERACY & HOW PATIENTS IMPROVE THEMSELVES

Interview with Russel L. Rothman, professor of health policy at Vanderbilt University Medical Center (VUMC):

> "*The good physician treats the disease; the great physician treats the patient who has the disease.*" —William Osler

The great health system treats the patient and their community to improve their health. It is very important to expand our view. Currently, VUMC is involved in the Medicare-transforming clinical practice initiative and over four thousand clinicians have been engaged across the southern

US.[451] It is a wide array of practices from small (one to two) clinical practices in rural areas to larger academic practices and has both primary care practices, safety net practices, and specialty practices in the collaboration. This initiative is involved in going out to each of these practices to teach them about how to provide more value-based healthcare— teaching how to measure quality metrics, how to report on quality metrics, and how to use these metrics to go through rapid cycles of quality improvements (not only to try to improve quality and utilization metrics to provide more value-based care for their communities, but also working with these practices to become patient-centered medical homes). Part of this is teaching about the importance of addressing social and behavioral determinants of health, including the importance of engaging families and the community to improve individual and population health. These practices can engage in their local communities, health systems, other clinical practices to tangibly improve care for their local community.

In recent years, there has been a proliferation of population health management programs introduced. Many of these programs attempt to identify a high-risk population and then promote interventions to reduce costs and improve health. Some of the programs have been successful, yet many have not been or remain unproven. Likely one factor that can sometimes explain why a program is not successful is when programs do not adequately account for and address the importance of social and behavioral determinants of

---

451 Matt Schorr, "VHAN awarded $28 million contract for Transforming Clinical Practice Initiative," *Vanderbilt University Medical Center*, September 29, 2015.

health that are ever so common today. When such practices or health systems do not take in such information and have strong, robust ways to address those determinants, that is when they fail. One factor of particular pertinence that can be addressed by clinicians, clinics, and health systems is that of health communication and how it can be used to engage patients and the community at large to improve individual and population health.

Over the recent past few decades, the US healthcare system has been increasingly complex—patients are sicker, they are on more medications, often with complex regimens, and yet hospitalizations are often shorter than ever before; clinic visits are shorter, and there is greater responsibility put on patients and their families to do a lot of tasks to take care of their health.[452] This is a daunting task for most Americans who are not familiar with how to handle complex healthcare issues.

Studies suggest that only about 50 percent of patients can tell you their discharge diagnosis and treatment plans after they go home from the hospital: patients can only recall about 20 percent of what is said to them at a clinic visit after they leave and go home.[453] This can be particularly challenging for patients who have lower health literacy skills. Over ninety million adults in the United States have only basic or below basic health literacy skills.[454] Over 110 million adults have poor

---

452 Ibid.

453 Matt Schorr, "VHAN awarded $28 million contract for Transforming Clinical Practice Initiative," *Vanderbilt University Medical Center*, September 29, 2015.

454 Ibid.

quantitative skills.[455] Over 20–30 million adults have limited English proficiency—patients who do not speak English as their first language.[456] The average American reads at about the eighth-grade level, and typically their quantitative skills are lower than that of an eighth-grade level.[457]

When many of us hear the word *literacy*, we typically think whether or not one can read. However, literacy includes a host of different skills—cultural and conceptual knowledge, listening and speaking skills (oral literacy), writing and reading skills (print literacy), and quantitative skills.[458] Literacy, overarchingly, is a functional skill—the ability for a patient or family member to read or be told to take information in, process the information, and then finally act on that information in an appropriate way.[459] Many patients, even those with good literacy skills, have a difficult time navigating and understanding our complex healthcare system. Moreover, it is important to understand the medical recommendations and health information provided to them.

Quantitative skills are particularly important because in health, a lot of numbers are used when communicating with patients. Talking about doses of medicine, blood sugar reading,

---

455 Matt Schorr, "VHAN awarded $28 million contract for Transforming Clinical Practice Initiative," *Vanderbilt University Medical Center*, September 29, 2015.

456 Ibid.

457 Matt Schorr, "VHAN awarded $28 million contract for Transforming Clinical Practice Initiative," *Vanderbilt University Medical Center*, September 29, 2015.

458 Ibid.

459 Matt Schorr, "VHAN awarded $28 million contract for Transforming Clinical Practice Initiative," *Vanderbilt University Medical Center*, September 29, 2015.

blood pressure reading, portion sizes, risks of procedures, and probability can be very challenging and frankly intimidating for many of the patients who really dislike numbers. Studies show patients struggle with medical forms, prescription labels, how to measure and adjust medications, issues involving the risk of probability, and other tasks.[460] It is known patients with lower health literacy skills have worse knowledge of their disease, lower self-care skills, worse clinical outcomes, and higher rates of mortality.[461] Literacy predicts health status even after adjusting other factors such as education level, socioeconomic background, or insurance status.[462]

To help combat this problem, it is imperative clinicians and health systems improve their communication to patients and families—which is especially important in building health systems that can engage patients, families, and communities to improve health. As health systems, it is important to consider how patients can access and navigate hospitals and clinics, how patients and families can figure out how to contact hospitals when there is a problem, how patients can figure out where to go when there is an appointment, and how patients can understand instructions given to them when they are discharged from the hospital.

Health systems are often in a bubble, with the thought that patients will come to them. This is simply not the case. In the United States, people, on average, spend 99.9 percent of their

---

460 Ibid.

461 Matt Schorr, "VHAN awarded $28 million contract for Transforming Clinical Practice Initiative," *Vanderbilt University Medical Center*, September 29, 2015.

462 Ibid.

time outside of the hospital.[463] Thus, it is important to consider approaches that can allow for outreach to communities and use good principles of health communication to understand their challenges and barriers to help them to address these barriers to improve their health. In the process of building these asynchronous forms of patient interaction, it is important to consider how patients interact with these tools. As health apps and telemedicine are being developed, there is a need to reach out to the community and understand what their needs are and what they understand, and they need to be participating in the development of these tools so they are targeted to the right people who can understand and use them to improve their health. There is also a need to consider issues of language, culture, and other challenges when patients may be using these tools. At the same time, there are several significant opportunities for health systems to partner with community organizations to reach out to the community and understand the needs the community has to help develop these targeted interventions to help the communities to improve individual and population health.

The transformation to a value-based healthcare system is a great opportunity to be like Sir William Osler—to treat the patient and not just the disease.

FORMING HABITS

We are creatures of habit. We follow the same patterns each and every day, for the most part. We brush our teeth, eat breakfast, and go to work.

---

463 Matt Schorr, "VHAN awarded $28 million contract for Transforming Clinical Practice Initiative," *Vanderbilt University Medical Center*, September 29, 2015.

What exactly makes it so hard to cultivate new healthy habits?

According to neuroscientists studying the formation of habits, it is the approach that is at fault.[464] We are, in short, unrealistic with our expectations, having lofty goals but not the bandwidth to execute those goals.

Here, I provide data-backed means of cultivating healthy habits.

First, you should aim to form habits based on pre-existing ones.[465] For instance, you may decide to add a new habit to a rigid scheduled portion of your day to make that new habit just as consistent.

Brian Jeffrey Fogg, an American social scientist at Stanford University, emphasizes the importance of starting with low-commitment habits before adding additional or more involved ones in his book, *Tiny Habits*.[466]

Phillippa Lally, a researcher at University College London, conducted a study in 2009 to understand the habit-formation process.[467] There were ninety-six volunteers who chose an eating or drinking activity to do on a daily basis in the

---

464 Elliot T. Berkman, "The Neuroscience of Goals and Behavior Change," *Journal of Consulting and Clinical Psychology* 70, no. 1, March 1, 2019.

465 Ibid.

466 BJ Fogg, *Tiny Habits: The Small Changes That Change Everything* (Boston: HMH Books, 2019).

467 Phillippa Lally, Cornelia H. M. van Jaarsveld, Henry W. W. Potts, and Jane Wardle, "How are habits formed: Modeling habit formation in the real world," *European Journal of Social Psychology* 40, no. 6, July 16, 2009.

same exact context. Every day, each volunteer filled out a self-report habit index where they recorded whether or not they executed that particular habit that day.[468] The study showed that performing a behavior on a more consistent basis showed a better model fit.[469] Moreover, it was found that it takes between 18 and 254 days for a task to become a habit, with the median being 66 days![470]

The lesson here is that habits take time to develop; by pursuing a task with increased frequency, that task can become a habit faster than otherwise.

In 1981, Ron Van Houten worked on a study altering the timing of elevator doors such that it took longer for the elevator doors to close.[471] This delay was enough to convince people that stairs are easier to take.[472] This shows just how sensitive we are.

Reward yourself when you follow through on a habit. Generally, it is ideal if this reward is an intermediate one because this can be more directly related to the habit rather than to the pleasure of that reward predominantly. Developing healthy

---

468 Ibid.

469 Phillippa Lally, Cornelia H. M. van Jaarsveld, Henry W. W. Potts, and Jane Wardle, "How are habits formed: Modeling habit formation in the real world," *European Journal of Social Psychology* 40, no. 6, July 16, 2009.

470 Ibid.

471 Ron Van Houten, Paul A. Nau, and Michael Merrigan, "Reducing Elevator Energy Use: A Comparison of Posted Feedback and Reduced Elevator Convenience," *Journal of Applied Behavioral Analysis* 14, no. 4, 1981.

472 Ibid.

habits can enable *you*, as the patient, to take charge of your health and be curious about all that goes behind the scenes.

CONCLUSION
- Personalized medical care:

    - A shift to at-home care as the default system: a patient needs to earn their way up to a level of sickness to be treated in a hospital setting.

    - A solid care network: there is a dire need to go beyond the paradigm of having specialists and shift toward having a multifaceted care team.

    - Big data and high-performance computing: some of the means of building predictive individualized algorithms.

- Healthy habits:

    - You should aim to form habits based on pre-existing ones.

    - Habits take time to develop; by pursuing a task with increased frequency, that task can become a habit faster than otherwise.

    - Reward yourself when you follow through on a habit.

CONCLUSION

So that was a lot of information; I know. I really hope that now you feel empowered to use this knowledge to fix the inequities that you see affecting either you or your loved ones. We started with covering how American healthcare began, then we transitioned into the principles of a top-tier healthcare system, and we concluded with tangible resolutions for YOU to make a positive difference.

In **Part I**, I shared how American healthcare got started and where along the way entanglements arose leading to the mess we are in today. I then provided an in-depth analysis of what patient autonomy and agency look like today, concluding with a discussion of how the COVID-19 pandemic shed light on healthcare disparities and a few of my policy proposals.

In **Part II**, I shared the standards of a top-tier healthcare system, emphasizing the importance of not falling for the "certainty epidemic," the necessity of achieving openness and national discussion, and the principles of a value-based system.

In **Part III**, I shared tangible resolutions for the vast array of American healthcare members. Starting with the pharmaceutical industry, I discussed how healthcare disparities are ever so present through the exorbitant pricing of pharmaceuticals along with a few tangible resolutions. I then spoke directly to the health insurance industry and provided a detailed explanation for tangible resolutions. Next, I spoke to the healthcare executives on increasing accessibility by tangible resolutions on reducing cost of care without compromising on the quality of care. Lastly, I spoke to all of you on a patient level.

Navigating the healthcare industry is no easy feat. With that said, it is important to recognize that YOU can make a difference.

As I write this book, I hope to distill the vast array of information I have presented by sharing some of my personal future plans as a patient and a future healthcare provider.

As a patient, I have learned the importance of being curious about your care. Some of the principles I share about *autonomy* are particularly relevant here. The more you share with your provider, the more context they have to work with, thereby leading to both a better quality of care and a better doctor–patient relationship, which can be very helpful for future visits.

Looking into the future, I am seeking to enter the field of medicine as a medical doctor. As a future healthcare provider, I believe that speaking with easy-to-understand language, a genuine desire to understand your patient—both from a medical and a humanistic viewpoint—and creating an atmosphere of encouraging a fruitful dialogue on the patient's medical care is of utmost importance.

With the research, interviews from leaders in the healthcare industry, and from countless patients that I have discussed in excruciating detail throughout this book, I hope with utmost sincerity that YOU can take this prescription to fix American healthcare.

ACKNOWLEDGMENTS

I would like to thank the following individuals for their contributions in helping me write this book.

PREORDERING:

Harsh Anand	Navjeet Bhullar
Nitin Dua	Ayush G Iyer
Kamlesh Shirpurkar	Eric Koester
Om Gautam	Neelkamal Agarwal
C Pohane	Mukesh Basandani
Zachary Desai	Bryan Munoz
Samantha Carter	Niraj Dhote
Anna Lenaker	Subhayan Basu

ADDITIONAL WORD OF THANKS:

Dr. Stephen Sonnenberg	Zoran Maksimovic
Dr. Thomas R. Frieden	Gjorgji Pejkovski
Dr. Mario Molina	Kristy Carter
Dan Ross (Health Rosetta)	Brian Bies
Stefan Larsson	Lyn S
Michael Porter	Jamie T.
Russel L. Rothman	Casey Mahalik
Dr. Paul B. Rothman	Heather Gomez
Kevin Bai	Judy Rosen
Pravik Tarala	Amita Bhasin
Dr. Kenneth Brewer	Anju Verma
Dr. Dohyeong Kim	Aruna Bhasin
Dr. Brit Berrett	Renu Bhatia
Mr. Jerry Grizzle	Savita Kohli
Mr. David Lyons	Ritu Anand Jagga
Chiu, Pak Kiu Harrison	Ayesha Rahul Bhasin
Anuradha Anand	Upasana Arora
Pratik Anand	Babita Verma
New Degree Press	Mansi Arora
Creator Institute Program at Georgetown University	Arun Saini
Natalie Bailey	

APPENDIX

INTRODUCTION: DO YOU SINCERELY WANT TO UNDERSTAND AMERICAN HEALTHCARE?

Braveman, Paula, and Laura Gottlieb. "The Social Determinants of Health: It's Time to Consider the Causes of the Causes." *Public Health Reports* 129, no. 2 (2014): 19-31.
https://www.ncbi.nlm.nih.gov/pmc/articles/PMC3863696/.

"CMS Office of the Actuary Releases 2018 National Health Expenditures." *Centers for Medicare & Medicaid Services*. December 5, 2019.
https://www.cms.gov/newsroom/press-releases/cms-office-actuary-releases-2018-national-health-expenditures.

Kamal, Rabah, Glorlando Ramirez, and Cynthia Cox. "How does health spending in the U.S. compare to other countries?" *Peterson-KFF Health System Tracker*, December 23, 2020.
https://www.healthsystemtracker.org/chart-collection/health-spending-u-s-compare-countries/#item-start.

Stiver, Ingrid. "What's likely to drive medical cost trend in 2019?" *PWC United States*, August 22, 2018.
https://www.pwc.com/us/en/industries/health-industries/library/hri-survey-2018.html.

Tikkanen, Roosa, and Milenda K. Abrams. "U.S. Health Care from a Global Perspective, 2019: Higher Spending, Worse Outcomes?" *The Commonwealth Fund*, January 30, 2020.
https://www.commonwealthfund.org/publications/issue-briefs/2020/jan/us-health-care-global-perspective-2019.

Tikkanen, Roosa, Robin Osborn, Elias Mossialos, Ana Djordjevic, and George A. Wharton. "International Health Care System Profiles Singapore." *The Commonwealth Fund*, June 5, 2020.
https://www.commonwealthfund.org/international-health-policy-center/countries/singapore.

Tolbert, Jennifer, and Kendal Orgera. "Key Facts about the Uninsured Population." *KFF*, November 6, 2020. https://www.kff.org/uninsured/issue-brief/key-facts-about-the-uninsured-population/.

CHAPTER I: HOW AMERICAN HEALTHCARE STARTED

Amadeo, Kimberly. "What is Obamacare?" *The Balance*, September 17, 2020. https://www.thebalance.com/what-is-obamacare-the-aca-and-what-you-need-to-know-3306065.

Cambridge Dictionary, s.v. "can't see the wood for the trees." accessed September 28, 2020. https://dictionary.cambridge.org/us/dictionary/english/can-t-see-the-wood-for-the-trees.

Davis, Elizabeth. "Diagnostic Related Grouping and How It Works." *verywellhealth*, November 26, 2020. https://www.verywellhealth.com/drg-101-what-is-a-drg-how-does-it-work-3916755.

Flexner, Abraham, and Herman Weiskotten Gates. *Flexner Report*. Princeton: Carnegie Foundation for the Advancement of Teaching, 1910.

Friedman, Milton. *Capitalism and Freedom*. Chicago: University of Chicago Press, 1962.

"History of SSA During the Johnson Administration 1963—1968." *Social Security*. https://www.ssa.gov/history/ssa/lbjmedicare1.html.

Ladd, Megan, and Vikas Gupta. "Cobra Laws and EMTALA." *StatPearls*, February 16, 2021. https://www.ncbi.nlm.nih.gov/books/NBK555935/.

McCulla, Theresa. "Medicine in Colonial North America." *Colonial North America at Harvard Library*, 2016. https://colonialnorthamerica.library.harvard.edu/spotlight/cna/feature/medicine-in-colonial-north-america

McGuff, Doug, and Robert P. Murphy. *Primal Prescription: Surviving the "Sick Care" Sinkhole*. Oxnard: Primal Blueprint Publishing, 2015.

Mihm, Stephen. "Employer-based health care was a wartime accident." *Chicago Tribune*, February 24, 2017. https://www.chicagotribune.com/opinion/commentary/ct-obamacare-health-care-employers-20170224-story.html.

Monheit, Alan C., Joel C. Cantor, Margaret Koller, and Kimberley S. Fox. "Community Rating and Sustainable Individual Health Insurance Markets in New Jersey." *Health Affairs* 23, no. 4 (2004). https://www.healthaffairs.org/doi/full/10.1377/hlthaff.23.4.167.

Shepherd, Gordon, and Cynthia Tsay. "Triumph and Tragedy: The Life of John Farquhar Fulton." *Harvey Cushing/John Hay Whitney Medical Library*. https://library.medicine.yale.edu/historical/fulton.

Stevens, Rosemary A. "Health Care in the Early 1960s." *Medicare & Medicaid Research Review* 18, no. 2, (1996).
https://www.ncbi.nlm.nih.gov/pmc/articles/PMC4193636/.

"The Final Report of the Committee on the Costs of Medical Care." *New England Journal of Medicine* 207, (1932).

CHAPTER II: TWENTY-FIRST CENTURY GOVERNMENTAL INTERVENTION

Amadeo, Kimberly. "What is Obamacare?" *The Balance*, September 17, 2020.
https://www.thebalance.com/what-is-obamacare-the-aca-and-what-you-need-to-know-3306065.

Monheit, Alan C., Joel C. Cantor, Margaret Koller, and Kimberley S. Fox. "Community Rating and Sustainable Individual Health Insurance Markets in New Jersey." *Health Affairs* 23, no. 4 (2004).
https://www.healthaffairs.org/doi/full/10.1377/hlthaff.23.4.167.

Wyckoff, Whitney Blair. "Number of Americans with Health Insurance Fell in 2009." *NPR*, September 16, 2010.
https://www.npr.org/sections/health-shots/2010/09/16/129908672/number-of-insured-americans-dropped-in-2009.

CHAPTER III: THE THEORY OF AUTONOMY

Aristotle. *Nicomachean Ethics Book VII: Symposium Aristotelicum*. Oxford: Oxford University Press, 2005.

Campana, A., F. Macciardi, O. Gambini, and S. Scarone. "The Wisconsin Card Sorting Test (WCST) performance in normal subjects: a twin study." *Neuropsychobiology* 14, no. 7 (1996).
https://pubmed.ncbi.nlm.nih.gov/8884753/.

Childress, James F., and Tom L. Beauchamp. *Principles of Biomedical Ethics 5th Edition*. (Oxford: Oxford University Press, 2001).

Grady, Patricia A., and Lisa Lucio Gough. "Self-Management: A Comprehensive Approach to Management of Chronic Conditions." *American Journal of Public Health* 14, no. 8 (August 2014).
https://www.ncbi.nlm.nih.gov/pmc/articles/PMC4103232/.

Grisso, T., P.S. Appelbaum, and C. Hill-Fotouhi. "The MacCAT-T: a clinical tool to assess patients' capacities to make treatment decisions." *Psychiatric Services* 48, no. 11 (November 1997).
https://pubmed.ncbi.nlm.nih.gov/9355168/.

Kertesz, A., N. Nadkarni, W. Davidson, and A. W. Thomas. "The Frontal Behavioral Inventory in the differential diagnosis of frontotemporal dementia." *Journal of the International Neuropsychological Society* 6, no. 4 (May 2000).
https://pubmed.ncbi.nlm.nih.gov/10902415/.

Mental Capacity Act. *NHS* 27. (January 2021).
https://www.nhs.uk/conditions/social-care-and-support-guide/making-decisions-for-someone-else/mental-capacity-act/.

Rendon, Adriana and Knut Schakel. "Psoriasis Pathogenesis and Treatment." *International Journal of Molecular Sciences* 20, no. 6 (March 2019).
https://www.ncbi.nlm.nih.gov/pmc/articles/PMC6471628/.

Varelius, Jukka. "The value of autonomy in medical ethics." *Medicine, Health Care, and Philosophy* 9, no. 3 (December 2006).
https://www.ncbi.nlm.nih.gov/pmc/articles/PMC2780686/.

CHAPTER IV: A MULTIDIMENSIONAL APPROACH TO PATIENT AUTONOMY

Aristotle. *Nicomachean Ethics Book VII: Symposium Aristotelicum*. Oxford: Oxford University Press, 2005.

Campana, A., F. Macciardi, O. Gambini, and S. Scarone. "The Wisconsin Card Sorting Test (WCST) performance in normal subjects: a twin study." *Neuropsychobiology* 14 no. 7 (1996).
https://pubmed.ncbi.nlm.nih.gov/8884753/.

Childress, James F., and Tom L. Beauchamp. *Principles of Biomedical Ethics 5th Edition*. (Oxford: Oxford University Press, 2001).

Grady, Patricia A., and Lisa Lucio Gough. "Self-Management: A Comprehensive Approach to Management of Chronic Conditions." *American Journal of Public Health* 14, no. 8, (August 2014).
https://www.ncbi.nlm.nih.gov/pmc/articles/PMC4103232/.

Grisso, T., P.S. Appelbaum, and C. Hill-Fotouhi. "The MacCAT-T: a clinical tool to assess patients' capacities to make treatment decisions." *Psychiatric Services* 48, no. 11, (November 1997).
https://pubmed.ncbi.nlm.nih.gov/9355168/.

A., Kertesz, N. Nadkarni, W. Davidson, and A. W. Thomas. "The Frontal Behavioral Inventory in the differential diagnosis of frontotemporal dementia." *Journal of the International Neuropsychological Society* 6, no. 4, (May 2000).
https://pubmed.ncbi.nlm.nih.gov/10902415/.

Rendon, Adriana, and Knut Schakel. "Psoriasis Pathogenesis and Treatment." *International Journal of Molecular Sciences* 20, no. 6, (March 2019).
https://www.ncbi.nlm.nih.gov/pmc/articles/PMC6471628/.

CHAPTER V: CASE STUDY—PATIENT AUTONOMY

Varelius, Jukka. "The value of autonomy in medical ethics." *Medicine, Health Care, and Philosophy* 9, no. 3, (December 2006).
https://www.ncbi.nlm.nih.gov/pmc/articles/PMC2780686/.

CHAPTER VI: HEALTH SYSTEM IN FLUX
Mental Capacity Act. *NHS* 27. (January 2021).
https://www.nhs.uk/conditions/social-care-and-support-guide/making-decisions-for-someone-else/mental-capacity-act/.

CHAPTER VII: THE CERTAINTY EPIDEMIC
Cherry, Kendra. "The 6 Types of Basic Emotions and Their Effect on Human Behavior." *verywellmind*, January 13, 2020.
https://www.verywellmind.com/an-overview-of-the-types-of-emotions-4163976.

"Flight Safety, discipline, and importance of checklists." *BAA Training*. September 25, 2017.
https://www.baatraining.com/flight-safety-discipline-and-importance-of-checklists/#:~:text=In%20aviation%2C%20a%20pre%2Dflight,for%20malfunctions%2C%20and%20for%20emergencies.

"Full Scorecard of India vs Pakistan Final 1985/86—Score Report." *ESPN cricinfo*.
https://www.espncricinfo.com/series/austral-asia-cup-1985-86-60863/india-vs-pakistan-final-65816/full-scorecard.

"Historical Snapshot." *Boeing*.
https://www.boeing.com/history/products/b-17-flying-fortress.page.

"Napoleon Bonaparte." *History.com*. November 9, 2009.
https://www.history.com/topics/france/napoleon.

"Reading Comprehension Strategies." *Division of Academic Enhacement University of Georgia*.
https://dae.uga.edu/resources/asg/reading_comprehension/strategies/.

Zeveloff, Julie. "There's a brilliant reason why Van Halen asked for a bowl of M&Ms with all the brown candies removed before every show." *Insider*. September 6, 2016.
https://www.insider.com/van-halen-brown-m-ms-contract-2016-9.

CHAPTER VIII: ACHIEVING OPENNESS AND NATIONAL DISCUSSION
"Artificial pancreas helps children with type 1 diabetes." *National Institutes of Health*. September 15, 2020.
https://www.nih.gov/news-events/nih-research-matters/artificial-pancreas-helps-children-type-1-diabetes.

Beckfield, Jason, and Clare Bambra. "Shorter lives in stingier states: Social policy shortcomings help explain the US mortality disadvantage." *ScienceDirect* 171, (October 18, 2016).
https://www.sciencedirect.com/science/article/pii/S0277953616305858.

Bradley, E., H. Sipsma, H., and L.A. Taylor. "American health care paradox - high spending on health care and poor health." *QJM: An International Journal of Medicine* 110, no. 2, (October 24, 2016).
https://academic.oup.com/qjmed/article/110/2/61/2681813.

Cooper, Cyrus, Cottrell, Elizabeth Taveras, Elsie M. and Maynika V. Rastogi, Maynika V. "The First 1,000 Days: Early Life Determinants of Chronic Disease." *Endocrine News*, July 2014.
https://endocrinenews.endocrine.org/july-2014-the-first-1000-days-early-life-determinants-of-chronic-disease-fix/.

Goodman, John. "Consumer Directed Health Care." *Networks Financial Institute at Indiana State University*. December 2006.
https://www.indstate.edu/business/sites/business.indstate.edu/files/Docs/2006-PB-20_Goodman.pdf.

"Health and Economic Costs of Chronic Diseases." *Centers for Disease Control and Prevention*, January 12, 2021.
https://www.cdc.gov/chronicdisease/about/costs/index.htm.

Landro, Laura. "Preventing the tragedy of misdiagnosis." *Pittsburgh Post-Gazette*. November 28, 2006.
https://www.post-gazette.com/news/health/2006/11/29/Preventing-the-tragedy-of-misdiagnosis/stories/200611290197.

"Life expectancy at birth (years)." *United Nations Development Programme Human Development Reports*. 2013.
http://hdr.undp.org/en/69206.

"Medicare Telemedicine Health Care Provider Fact Sheet." *Centers for Medicare & Medicaid Services*. March 17, 2020.
https://www.cms.gov/newsroom/fact-sheets/medicare-telemedicine-health-care-provider-fact-sheet.

Mercieca-Bebber, Rebecca, Madeleine T. Calvert King, Melanie J. Stockler, R. Martin, and Michael Friedlander. "The importance of patient-reported outcomes in clinical trials and strategies for future optimization." *Dovepress Patient Related Outcome Measures* 9, (November 1, 2018).
https://www.ncbi.nlm.nih.gov/pmc/articles/PMC6219423/.

Perry, Susan. "U.S. life expectancy ranking will plummet by 2040, researchers predict." *MinnPost*, October 19, 2018.
https://www.minnpost.com/second-opinion/2018/10/u-s-life-expectancy-ranking-will-plummet-by-2040-researchers-predict/.

Roser, Max, Ortiz-Ospina, Esteban, and Hannah Ritchie. "Life Expectancy." *Our World in Data*. 2013.
https://ourworldindata.org/life-expectancy.

Steward, Walter, F. Shah, Nirav R. Selna, Mark J. Paulus, Ronald A. and James M. Walker. "Bridging the Inferential Gap: The Electronic Health Record and Clinical Evidence Emerging tools can help physicians bridge the gap between knowledge they possess and knowledge they do not." *Health Affairs* 26, no. 2, (January 26, 2007).
https://www.ncbi.nlm.nih.gov/pmc/articles/PMC2670472/.

Toffolutti, Veronica, and David Stuckler. "A Culture of Openness Is Associated With Lower Mortality Rates Among 137 English National Health Service Acute Trusts." *Health Affairs* 38, no. 5, (May 2019).
https://www.healthaffairs.org/doi/abs/10.1377/hlthaff.2018.05303.

Troy Segal, "Decision Support System—DSS." *Investopedia*. June 27, 2020.
https://www.investopedia.com/terms/d/decision-support-system.asp.

CHAPTER IX: PRINCIPLES OF A VALUE-BASED SYSTEM

"HEDIS and Performance Management." *NCQA*.
https://www.ncqa.org/hedis/.

"Mandatory Reporting of Infectious Diseases by Clinicians." *CDC*. June 22, 1990.
https://www.cdc.gov/mmwr/preview/mmwrhtml/00001665.htm.

"What Matters Most: Patient Outcomes and the Transformation of Health Care." *ICHOM*.
https://ichom.org/files/books/ICHOM_Book.pdf.

CHAPTER X: A PAINFUL PILL TO SWALLOW

Fernando, Jason. "Gross Domestic Product (GDP)." *Investopedia*. November 13, 2020.
https://www.investopedia.com/terms/g/gdp.asp#:~:text=Gross%20domestic%20
product%20(GDP)%20is,a%20given%20country's%20economic%20health.

Frieden, Thomas R., Cherian V. Varghese, Sandeep P. Kishore, Norman R.C. Campbell, Andrew E. Moran, Raj Padwal, and Marc G. Jaffe. "Scaling up effective treatment of hypertension—A pathfinder for universal health coverage." *The Journal of Clinical Hypertension 21*, no. 10, (September 23, 2019).
https://onlinelibrary.wiley.com/doi/full/10.1111/jch.13655.

Jung, Emily, Alfred H. Engelberg, and Aaron S. Kesselheim. "Do large pharma companies provide drug development innovation? Our analysis says no." *Statnews*. December 10, 2019.
https://www.statnews.com/2019/12/10/large-pharma-companies-provide-little-new-drug-development-innovation/.

Lee, Kristen. "Current Procedural Terminology (CPT) Code." *SearchHealthIT*. June 2015.
https://searchhealthit.techtarget.com/definition/Current-Procedural-Terminology-CPT.

"Major Recurring Reports." *Congressional Budget Office*.
https://www.cbo.gov/about/products/major-recurring-reports.

"Pharbetol Extra Strength Coupons & Prices." *SingleCare*.
https://www.singlecare.com/prescription/pharbetol-extra-strength.

"Poll: Nearly 1 in 4 Americans Taking Prescription Drugs Say It's Difficult to Afford Their Medicines, including Larger Shares Among Those with Health Issues, with Low Incomes and Nearing Medicare Age." *KFF*. March 1, 2019.
https://www.kff.org/health-costs/press-release/poll-nearly-1-in-4-americans-taking-prescription-drugs-say-its-difficult-to-afford-medicines-including-larger-shares-with-low-incomes/.

Starling, Naureen, John Neoptolemos, and David Cunningham. "Role of erlotinib in the management of pancreatic cancer." *Dovepress Therapeutics and Clinical Risk Management 2*, no. 4, (December 2006).
https://www.ncbi.nlm.nih.gov/pmc/articles/PMC1936363/.

Tikkanen, Roosa Osborn, Robin Mossialos, Elias Djordjevic, Ana Wharton, George A. "International Health Care System Profiles Singapore." *The Commonwealth Fund*, June 5, 2020.
https://www.commonwealthfund.org/international-health-policy-center/countries/singapore.

Webb, Lori-Lynne A. "Note similarities and differences between HCPCS, CPT codes." *HCPRO*. September 5, 2012.
https://www.hcpro.com/HIM-284009-8160/Note-similarities-and-differences-between-HCPCS-CPT-codes.html#:~:text=The%20Q%20codes%20are%20used,codes%20for%20claims%20processing%20purposes.

CHAPTER XI: A PRIMER ON HEALTH INSURANCE

Bal, B. Sonny. "An Introduction to Medical Malpractice in the United States." *Clinical Orthopaedics and Related Research* 467, no. 2, (November 26, 2008). https://www.ncbi.nlm.nih.gov/pmc/articles/PMC2628513/.

Faley, Kevin G., and Andrea M. Alonso. "High-low Agreements: Misunderstood Litigation Technique." *MDAF*. March 27, 1998.
https://mdafny.com/index.aspx?TypeContent=CUSTOMPAGEARTICLE&custom_pages_articlesID=14799.

CHAPTER XII: THE AFFORDABILITY SCALE

Cohen, Robin A., and Emily P. Zammitti. "High-deductible Health Plan Enrollment Among Adults Aged 18–64 With Employment-based Insurance Coverage." *Centers for Disease Control and Prevention*. August 2018.
https://www.cdc.gov/nchs/products/databriefs/db317.htm.

Morrisey, Michael A. and Kosali Simon. "The Compensation and Productivity of Health Economists: Results of the 2018 Survey of ASHEcon Membership." *ASHEcon*, June 24, 2019.
https://ashecon.confex.com/ashecon/2019/webprogram/Session3317.html.

Ritchie, Melissa. "Kaiser Permanente creates COVID-19 Social Health Playbook." *Kaiser Permanente*, October 13, 2020.
https://about.kaiserpermanente.org/community-health/news/kaiser-permanente-creates-covid-19-social-health-playbook.

Saad, Lydia. "More Americans Delaying Medical Treatment Due to Cost." *Gallup*, December 9, 2019.
https://news.gallup.com/poll/269138/americans-delaying-medical-treatment-due-cost.aspx.

CHAPTER XIII: WHAT YOU CAN DO TO FIX THE HEALTHCARE SYSTEM AS A PATIENT

Berkman, Elliot T. "The Neuroscience of Goals and Behavior Change." *Journal of Consulting and Clinical Psychology* 70, no. 1, (March 1, 2019).
https://www.ncbi.nlm.nih.gov/pmc/articles/PMC5854216/.

Fogg, BJ. *Tiny Habits: The Small Changes That Change Everything.* Boston: HMH Books, 2019.

Chalmers, Iain. "Why the 1948 MRC trial of streptomycin used treatment allocation based on random numbers." *Journal of the Royal Society of Medicine* 104, no. 9, (September 2011).

"History of Hospitals." *PennNursing, University of Pennsylvania.* https://www.nursing.upenn.edu/nhhc/nurses-institutions-caring/history-of-hospitals/.

Houten, Ron, Paul A. Van Nau, and Michael Merrigan. "Reducing Elevator Energy Use: A Comparison of Posted Feedback and Reduced Elevator Convenience." *Journal of Applied Behavioral Analysis* 14, no. 4, (1981). http://www.behaviorpedia.com/wp-content/uploads/2014/06/Posted-feedback-reduced-convenience-and-elevator-energy-use-Van-Houten-et-al.-JABA-14-1981-377.pdf.

Lally, Phillippa, Cornelia H. Jaarsveld, Henry M. van Potts, and Jane Wardle. "How are habits formed: Modeling habit formation in the real world." *European Journal of Social Psychology* 40, no. 6, (July 16, 2009). https://onlinelibrary.wiley.com/doi/abs/10.1002/ejsp.674.

Schorr, Matt. "VHAN awarded $28 million contract for Transforming Clinical Practice Initiative." *Vanderbilt University Medical Center*, September 29, 2015. https://www.meharry-vanderbilt.org/all-news-research-news/vhan-awarded-28-million-contract-transforming-clinical-practice-initiative.

www.ingramcontent.com/pod-product-compliance
Lightning Source LLC
LaVergne TN
LVHW011822060526
838200LV00053B/3874